China, South Korea, and the Socotra Rock Dispute

Senan Fox

China, South Korea, and the Socotra Rock Dispute

A Submerged Rock and Its Destabilizing Potential

palgrave
macmillan

Senan Fox
Kanazawa University
Kanazawa, Japan

ISBN 978-981-13-2076-7 ISBN 978-981-13-2077-4 (eBook)
https://doi.org/10.1007/978-981-13-2077-4

Library of Congress Control Number: 2018952943

This Palgrave Pivot imprint is published by the registered company Springer Nature Singapore Pte Ltd.
The registered company address is: 152 Beach Road, #21-01/04 Gateway East, Singapore 189721, Singapore

To my parents, Anna and John

Think where man's glory most begins and ends, and say my glory was I had such friends.

William Butler Yeats

Preface

Writing a book about an under-explored Sino-South Korean maritime dispute was not an easy task, but the linguistic and research challenges that faced me were ultimately overcome. Initially, the work was a product of research conducted at the University of Tokyo, as part of a post-doctoral research fellowship there. Funded by the Japan Society for the Promotion of Science (JSPS), that project followed on from my Ph.D. thesis, which tackled the question of why bilateral approaches to the East China Sea disagreements between Japan and China have a tendency to fluctuate. It also complemented my September 2016 "China Information" (Sage) journal article which contrasted the influence of popular sentiment and domestic politics on the Okinotorishima dispute in the Western Pacific and the Senkaku Shoto/Diaoyu Islands dispute in the East China Sea. As with these earlier works, a central goal of this book was to identify the main causal factors, to draw lessons from the research, to reflect on the possibilities of a resolution, and to pen proposals for the manageability of the dispute. The book's release is also timely as it comes in a period of unpredictable and often sudden fluctuations in relations between the two Koreas as well as their ties with China and the USA.

Socotra Rock is an underwater rock that is located between mainland China and the Korean Peninsula in waters that straddle the Yellow Sea and the East China Sea. For reasons explained inside, the dispute is not a territorial question but rather one related to jurisdictional rights in the sea area in which the feature rests. This work was motivated by a desire to present to East Asia watchers an insight into an under-examined maritime dispute involving two major players in the region, China and South Korea.

An added inspiration was to contribute to the increasingly important study of sea-related disagreements and their relevance to national security, domestic politics, and international law, as well as to the buzzwords in maritime inter-state relations: resource competition and freedom of navigation. Much has been written to date on the South China Sea disputes as well as the East China Sea disputes with more needing to be said about this issue at the gateway to the Yellow Sea, in close proximity to the People's Republic of China (PRC)'s core urban, industrial, and military centers. This is not to mention its strategic importance to South Korea.

Although the rock has been a bilateral issue for over half a century, the aggravation of the Socotra Rock dispute is also a relatively recent yet no less important phenomenon with consequences for maritime disagreements in East Asia and elsewhere. Frictions regarding the feature have also been accompanied by wider regional developments related to China's rise and its greater capability and willingness to physically display its control and "rights" in disputed areas. They have also coincided with the construction of the nearby and massive Jeju Island naval base, which began in 2007 and was officially opened in 2016. To date, this is the only publication in monograph form that deals directly and chronologically with the dispute. Other shorter works often only focus on technical components, but this work also addresses the political, economic, historical, and present-day strategic implications.

My hope for this book is that readers will be more informed about this understated yet important issue of influence in terms of the challenges faced by the littoral states of East Asia. For China watchers, hopefully it will provide another important insight into that state's activities and strategy in waters it claims as its own. This work also presents evidence of more erratic behavior by the PRC in recent years, pointing readers perhaps to a portend of things to come: hence the decision to address the Socotra Rock issue. By reading the seven chapters contained herein, the reader should receive a solid grounding in regard to both relations over the rock prior to escalation in the early 2000s and developments after the early 2000s until the present day. The reader's knowledge of the role played by key factors such as security strategy, international law, and economic resources should likewise be enhanced. The destabilizing influence of bilateral challenges related to domestic politics, historical controversies, economic ties, popular nationalist sentiment, bureaucratic miscommunications, and a Chinese Air Defense Identification Zone (ADIZ) in November 2013 is also covered. It is my sincere wish that the reader will learn about the commonalities between the issues and will possess a greater appreciation of their utility for present and future policy prescription and analysis. In addition, I hope that insights into the dispute's impact upon bilateral and regional relations and why a resolution has proved elusive to date will be broadened.

As I introduce this book, allow me also to acknowledge those without whom the work may not have seen the light of day. These include my parents, John and Anna, whose unceasing love and support provided me with much needed emotional sustenance. Special thanks goes out also to the book's editor, Dr. Mary Jane Fox (no relation). She will never truly know how much her skill, patience, and refusal to give up in spite of looming deadlines was the determining factor in finalizing the book. I would also like to thank the JSPS, who provided me with all the necessary funding to come to Japan and to complete the research as a post-doctoral fellow. In particular, I wish to express my deepest gratitude to Professor Akio Takahara (Faculty of Law) at the University of Tokyo, who kindly agreed to act as my research host and who, throughout my time there, acted with the utmost professionalism and kindness with regard to my various requests and enquiries. Thanks also to the administrators and staff at the said Faculty of Law for all their assistance. Last but not least, I would like to thank my colleagues and the administrative staff at the School of International Studies at Kanazawa University for their advice and help as I endeavored to complete the book.

Kanazawa, Japan Senan Fox

Contents

Abbreviations

ABMD	Aegis Ballistic Missile Defense
ADIZ	Air Defense Identification Zone
AIS	Automatic Identification System
ASEAN	Association of Southeast Asian Nations
CCP	Chinese Communist Party
CCTV	China Central Television
CFR	Council on Foreign Relations
CLCS	Commission on the Limits of the Continental Shelf
DPRK	Democratic People's Republic of Korea
DRP	Defense Reform Plan
EEZs	Exclusive Economic Zones
FDI	Foreign Direct Investment
FIR	Flight Information Region
FONOP	Freedom of Navigation Operation
FTA	Free Trade Agreement
ICAO	International Civil Aviation Organization
ICJ	International Court of Justice
IORS	Ieodo Ocean Research Station
IUU	Illegal, Unreported, and Unregulated (fishing)
JADIZ	Japan Air Defense Identification Zone
JCS	Joint Chiefs of Staff (ROK)
JDZ	Joint Development Zone
JFC	Joint Fisheries Committee
JMSDF	Japanese Maritime Self-Defense Force
KADIZ	Korea Air Defense Identification Zone
KBS	Korean Broadcasting System
KCG	Korean Coast Guard

KCMGN	Korea Committee on Marine Geographical Names
KHOA	Korea Hydrographic and Oceanographic Administration
KIOST	Korean Institute of Ocean Science and Technology
KIPA	Korea Institute of Public Administration
KORDI	Korean Ocean Research and Development Institute
MOFAT	Ministry of Foreign Affairs and Trade (South Korea)
NEP	Northeast Project
NGO	Non-Governmental Organization
NLL	Northern Limit Line
PCA	Permanent Court of Arbitration
PLAAF	People's Liberation Army Air Force
PLAN	People's Liberation Army Navy
PMZ	Provisional Measures Zone
PRC	People's Republic of China
PWZ	Provisional Measures Zone
RNP	Revive Northeast Project
ROK	Republic of Korea
ROKAF	Republic Of Korea Air Force
ROKN	Republic Of Korea Navy
SAR	Search And Research (Exercises)
SIR	Society for Ieodo Research
SLOCs	Sea Lines of Communication
SOA	State Oceanic Administration
THAAD	Terminal High-Altitude Area Defense
TZ	Transitional Zone
UNCLOS	United Nations Convention on the Law of the Sea
UNESCO	United Nations Educational, Scientific and Cultural Organization
UNSC	United Nations Security Council

List of Maps

CHAPTER 1

An Insoluble Dispute?

Abstract This introductory chapter begins by describing the purpose of the book and briefly introduces the various contexts in which the Socotra Rock dispute is situated. It provides a broad overview of the complex difficulties related to solving the dispute. This includes a succinct overview of the role of international maritime law in advance of a more in-depth discussion in a subsequent chapter, as well as why tensions increased after the early 2000s, and the significance of this dispute for the wider Sino-South Korean relationship for East Asia and the international community in general. Given that topography and geographical context figure so fundamentally in this issue, they are described before proceeding to other issues, such as the disputed dividing line, Exclusive Economic Zones (EEZs), and continental shelf claims, and South Korea's contentious construction of a research station in 2003.

Keywords Socotra Rock dispute • Sino-South Korean relationship • East Asia • Exclusive Economic Zones (EEZs)

Introduction

Socotra Rock has been an object of tension between two East Asian states for many years, and no doubt will continue to be a problem in the future. It is one of several difficult maritime disputes involving China and a smaller state, and for which international maritime law offers no simple remedy.

S. Fox, *China, South Korea, and the Socotra Rock Dispute*,
https://doi.org/10.1007/978-981-13-2077-4_1

This book examines the decades-long Socotra Rock dispute between South Korea (Republic of Korea/ROK) and the People's Republic of China (PRC), which essentially revolves around a submerged feature in the northwest of the East China Sea,[1] and located between mainland China and the Korean Peninsula.

The ongoing disagreement has come to play a more prominent role in bilateral relations within the last 15 years, and this is mainly due to Seoul's construction of a research station on the feature in 2003. This in turn provoked a more assertive vocal and physical defense of Beijing's own claims in the area. Even though by 1996 many states had formally designated their Exclusive Economic Zones (EEZs) under the United Nations Convention on the Law of the Sea (UNCLOS) with subsequent exploration, resource extraction, and jurisdictional rights inside the said zones, this had not been resolved regarding Socotra Rock. After 2003, China responded to South Korea's construction on Socotra Rock by conducting surveillance activities in the area and then claiming jurisdiction over the feature in 2006 (Kim Young-jin, 18/09/2012). This escalated tensions and continues to the present.

Briefly, and in terms of international maritime law, this is a dispute over a submerged feature, thus not making it territorial or sovereignty-based in nature, but rather a question of which state has the right to exercise jurisdiction over it and the surrounding waters. Although the research station was built without consulting China, South Korea's position is that no prior agreement was necessary because 'Ieodo' is situated within South Korea's EEZ, and the zone is delimited using the internationally accepted median line approach to maritime demarcation. The rock, they argue, is also on South Korea's continental shelf, and as such, they contend that the station's construction was permissible (Roehrig, 2012: 74).

China's own stance is quite different. The aim is to demarcate the area via an extended natural prolongation of the continental shelf approach, or at the very least, one that takes into consideration China's size, population, coastline, and other factors. For this reason, Beijing claims that the feature lies within China's EEZ and is also on China's continental shelf in accordance with their view that the seabed area is Chinese and not South Korean. The shortcomings in China's continental shelf claims and indeed the contradictions in South Korea's continental shelf claims are discussed in detail in Chap. 2. The Chinese therefore believe that the research station should not have been built until the two sides agreed on a final demarcation of their respective EEZs and continental shelves.

The crux of the issue thus rests on questions regarding within which state's EEZ and on which state's continental shelf the feature rightfully rests according to international maritime law, specifically UNCLOS. Both states argue that existing maritime legislation favors their own respective positions and claims. It is clear, however, that while all states tend to select and choose articles and clauses which favor their own interests, in this case the PRC finds itself defending an outmoded stance and South Korea embracing a more widely accepted position for resolving the problem of overlapping EEZs. It must be pointed out that this embrace by Seoul has been selective. As presented herein, the issue is much more than an insignificant dispute over a worthless rock, but rather one which links into pressing questions regarding each state's security, economy, and domestic politics, as well as approaches to globally accepted laws and regulations regarding such disagreements. It also has ramifications for maritime disputes elsewhere in the region, such as in other parts of the East China Sea and in the South China Sea, where claimant states have found themselves at dangerous odds over how to properly demarcate overlapping sea territory.

In order to fully discuss the Socotra Rock dilemma, this book comprises seven chapters. This chapter provides an introduction and background, including topography, geographical location, its place in myth and legend, and finally historical background. Chapter 2 covers the legal disagreements and entanglements at the center of the dispute, which is crucial to understanding the lack of progress. Chapter 3 examines the influence of wider bilateral and regional challenges. It particularly notes the increasingly fraught nature of ties between the two neighbors since the early 2000s, when the optimism of the 1990s was replaced by more realism and mixed feelings. Pertinent controversies and agreements directly related to Socotra Rock since the late 1980s are discussed in detail in Chap. 4. In the following chapter (Chap. 5), the significance of China's controversial and somewhat overlooked Air Defense Identification Zone (ADIZ) declaration in November 2013 is examined in general and then specific to the Socotra Rock dispute. The inter-relationship between the Socotra Rock issue and security as well as domestic political and economic factors is under scrutiny in Chap. 6, including how they have tested and continue to test bilateral ties today and in recent years. Finally, Chap. 7 concludes with the future outlook for the issue, as well as some suggestions for dispute management and preventing the Socotra Rock disagreement from damaging the wider and economically prosperous bilateral relationship. Next, however, given that topography and geographical context figure so fundamentally into this issue, it is vital to describe these before proceeding to further discussions on the key issues.

Topography and Geographical Context

Socotra Rock is the internationally recognized English language name for a permanently submerged rock, its highest point at low tide being 4.6 m (15 feet) below sea level. It is situated in the northwest of the East China Sea and just at the southern end of the Yellow Sea (Korea Hydrographic and Oceanographic Agency, 2010). Looking at a map, it is located at latitude 32° 07′ 22.63″ North and longitude 125° 10′ 56.81″ East and appears to rest roughly equidistant between mainland China and the Korean Peninsula and at the entrance to the Yellow Sea. Its nearest neighbor is the South Korean island of Marado, just south of Jejudo or Jeju Island, 80.45 nautical miles (nmi) to its northeast. The nearest PRC territory is Haijiao Island, 133.3 nmi to its southwest,[2] and Sheshan Dao, one of the PRC's 'straight baseline claim' points, is 155 nmi away to the west.[3] The Japanese island of Torishima is located 148.4 nmi to the east of the feature (Surhone et al., 2010: 1; Korea Hydrographic and Oceanographic Agency, 2010).

Today, South Koreans generally refer to the submerged rock as Ieodo (Ieo Island), a term which inaccurately identifies the rock as an island. This name arguably reflects the feature's place in Korean maritime folklore as a mythical rather than an actual island. Individual Koreans as well as historical and contemporary Korean documents also refer to the feature as 'Parangdo'. In January 2001, the Korea Institute of Geology officially designated the feature 'Ieodo' (Surhone et al., 2010: 1–2). The Chinese, on the other hand, have historically referred to the submerged rock as 'Suyan Jiao' meaning Suyan Rock, Suyan Reef, or Suyan islet (Brunet-Jailly, 2015: 279). According to at least one Chinese language source, the name 'Suyan' derives from the underwater rock's *relative* proximity to Jiangsu Province (Su Yan jiao, 13/03/2012). English language and other international publications tend to refer to the feature as Socotra Rock, the name given to it after the British commercial ship *Socotra* recorded the rock on its charts in 1900 (Surhone et al., 2010: 1–2).

To emphasize just how elusive Socotra Rock is, as mentioned earlier, its highest peak stands just 4.6 m (2.51 fathoms) *below* the water line. This proximity to the surface has made the feature one that has claimed many an unsuspecting mariner over the centuries, and as such, has earned the rock a place in folklore and legend, predominantly Korean. It can actually be seen above water with the naked eye, but only in the stormiest of waters when the waves can reach up to 10 m high (Korea Hydrographic and Oceanographic Agency, 2010). The dangers to fishermen and mariners posed by the rock helped to spawn the traditional Korean saying that 'one who sees Parangdo can never return' because whoever saw the rock faced almost certain death amid the high waves and torrential rain. For such reasons, the feature was considered a type of Valhalla for the souls of drowned fishermen who ventured too far from port and thus resided on the mythical island beneath the waves forever, never to return (Surhone et al., 2010: 1–2; Baek Hee Youn, 14/08/2011) (Map 1.1).

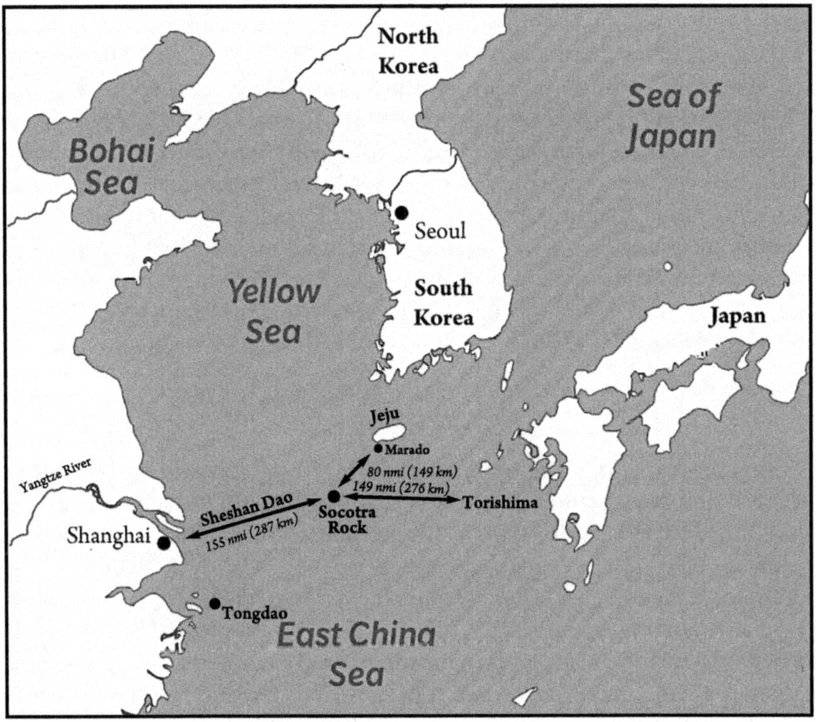

Map 1.1 Location of Socotra Rock

The rock covers a substantial area, extending 1.82 km from north to south and 1.4 km from east to west. At 40 m deep, it takes up an area of 600 m from north to south and 750 m from east to west. The feature is characterized by a very jagged structure in its higher southern and eastern sections, but with more gentle slopes to its lower north and west. Due to its irregular shape, the rock's depth from the surface ranges from 4.6 m at its shallowest point to 52 m at its deepest (Korea Hydrographic and Oceanographic Agency, 2010).

South Korea's Ieodo Ocean Research Station (IORS), which has been at the center of resurgent Sino-Korean disputes, sits at a depth of 41 m and is built upon less rugged foundations just 700 m to the south of the feature's peak (Korea Hydrographic and Oceanographic Agency, 2010). This weather station and observation facility with a helipad was built in 2003 at the behest of the Seoul government for the official purposes of improving their ability to monitor weather patterns, to protect and conserve fishery and environmental interests, and to measure ocean currents in the immediate area. It also serves as a lighthouse for over 250,000 vessels that pass through its surrounding waters every year (Shin Hae-in, 27/07/2011; "Conflict over the reef's jurisdiction", 03/02/2014). The facility is largely self-sufficient with its own wind generators, desalination machines, and a permanent crew of South Korean personnel. None of the publicly known facilities on the research station suggest that it will have a military purpose. This is despite the fact that Seoul indicated its intention to extend the South Korean Navy's reach and capabilities in the East China Sea via the construction of a naval base on nearby Jeju Island to the northeast (Van Dyke, 2011: 15).

Legend

Among Koreans, it is the more than 600,000 inhabitants of the nearby Marado and Jeju Islands who attach the greatest and indeed richest cultural and historical value to the submerged feature. This has been featured in historical records over the centuries. The Jeju islanders, for example, refer to the rock as 'Ieodo' due to their folklore, even though it is clearly an underwater islet.[4] In times past, the women of Jeju believed that Ieodo was the resting place for their loved ones lost at sea, a mystical rather than an actual island, and a place where families broken by maritime tragedies might possibly reunite. One locally known legend, later converted to a song still sung today by female Jeju divers, known as '*haenyeo*' (sea women), while at work, tells of a local woman and her father-in-law who went to sea in a rowboat looking for her lost and presumed drowned husband. Throughout the search, the fable tells of how the woman repeatedly sang the words 'Ieodosanna, Ieodosanna' ('*Is he living in Ieodo?, Is he living in Ieodo?*'). When the rowboat is led to Ieodo by the wind and the waves, the woman discovers her husband living there but already married to another woman (Baek Hee Youn, 14/08/2011). For the *haenyeo* of Jeju Island, Ieodo is, in historical memory, both an 'Island of Abundance', a place with rich fishing grounds and plentifully bestowed with sea mustard and abalone, and an 'Island of Grief', which claimed their husbands and other male relatives (Chin, 03/02/2014). Another version of this story tells of the husband abandoning his wife to live in Ieodo with his new mistress. After much persuasion, the woman and the man's father convince the man to return to Jeju. On the way back, however, their boat encounters a violent storm and they all drown (Korea Hydrographic and Oceanographic Agency, 2010; Baek Hee Youn, 14/08/2011). Yet another version of the legend tells of Ieodo being an island of widows at the time that the spirit of the drowned husband arrived there (Korea Hydrographic and Oceanographic Agency, 2010; Baek Hee Youn, 14/08/2011).

The feature's location mid-way between the Korean Peninsula and China also spawned numerous folk tales. One tells of an incident in the third year of King Chung Yeol's reign in the Goryeo Dynasty (918–1392) when the Jeju Islanders were forced to pay tribute to the Chinese every year. On one occasion, the tribute fleet never returned home, compelling a female relative of one of the deceased to compose a melancholic song which ended with the words 'Ah, Ah, Ieodo ya, Ieodo'. Another legend recalls a husband, Dongji Go, who was stranded on Ieodo and longed to be reunited with his wife, constantly looking to the horizon, and calling her name and singing to her from the 'seashore'. The story led to a tradition of people on passing vessels calling out his name to console him and singing a popular song inspired by the tale. In time, the legend tells of how the husband was rescued by a Chinese ship and returned to Jeju to live out his days in happiness. Jeju villagers referred to a woman who had accompanied Dongji Go as Yeodot or Grandmother of Ieodo. They revered her as a village goddess after her death and constructed an altar in her memory (Korea Hydrographic and Oceanographic Agency, 2010).

Other songs illustrated the feature's role as a marker on journeys to the outer, non-Korean world, to countries such as China and Japan: 'If you want to go to Kangnam (China), look ahead for Henam, Ieodo is halfway' (Chin, 03/02/2014). Socotra Rock has also been a feature in Korean literature. A notable example is the mystery novel *Iodo* (also *Ieodo*), which the leading novelist Lee Cheong-jun[5] wrote in 1974. The novel was later adapted into a movie in 1977 and tells the story of the reporter Chon's death during a naval expedition to the submerged rock (Song Sang-il, 2012: 129). According to a leading Ieodo activist, the Korean poet and scholar, Choi Yearn-hong, the lore of the rock's legend has, in addition to his own poetry, also inspired famous literary works such as Lee Cheong-jun's previously mentioned novel and Chang Il-hong's play 'Sea Woman Heading to Ieodo' (Choi, 25/06/2010). The Society of Ieodo Research has compiled an anthology of related poems prior to, and after, 2003, when the research station was constructed. A poem, 'Eodo', by the famous poet and Nobel Prize contender, Ko Un, is included in these collections (Song Sang-il, 2012: 148). In 2012, the government-sponsored Korea Institute of Public Administration (KIPA) published a book in English, *Korean Maritime Sovereignty*, which argued why both Japan and China were incorrect in their respective claims to both Dokdo (*Takeshima* in Japanese) and Ieodo. The book also asserted that the commonly named Sea of Japan should instead be known as the East Sea (Kang Hyun-kyung, 11/10/2012).

For Jeju islanders in particular, Socotra Rock has thus traditionally conjured up conflicting images of a place of doom and death alongside eternal peace, refuge, and the hope of reunion (Baek Hee Youn, 14/08/2011). While one might ask what such stories have to do with contemporary disputes over Socotra Rock, these legends are often cited to illustrate the Jeju and Marado Islanders' 'centuries-old deep-seated attachment to the rock', and to spur South Korean citizens to protect Ieodo (Kang Hyun-kyung, 10/12/2010). As Choi described it, Ieodo incorporates not just physical Korean territory, but it is also part of the Korean mindset and extends to the intellectual and cultural realm of the country's life (Choi, 25/06/2010). By emphasizing the feature's emotional and cultural value to the Korean people, these stories no doubt serve to buttress Seoul's claims in the area.

Historical Backdrop

In addition to myth, legend, and cultural expression attached to Socotra Rock, there is a long and significant history. This includes contrasting historical claims, including Chinese contentions that 'Suyan' was mentioned in an ancient classical Chinese text compiled in the fourth century

BCE. From there, more recent references from the Ming Dynasty (1368–1644) are offered, as well as the long history of Chinese, Dutch, French, Japanese, and Russian mapping and surveillance of adjacent waters since the 1600s. There is also evidence of China surveying the feature in the late 1800s, Japanese plans to build submarine facilities and a lighthouse in 1938, and the notable year of 1951 when post-war South Korea made its first formal claims. Thus the role of legend shares an important place with its counterpart, the historical record.

The oldest of the historical documents referred to is the ancient classical Chinese text about geography and legends, *Shan Hai Jing* (*The Classic of Mountains and Seas*), compiled at least 2300 years ago. A possible reference to the feature is made in mentioning a 'Su Rock', although it is not certain if this refers to the actual Socotra Rock of today. The text also refers to myths and legends throughout, making any factual link tenuous. The later Ming Dynasty nautical book *Shunfeng xiangsong* (*Voyage with a Tail Wind*), claimed to have been published in 1403, includes the line 'Ancient Japanese come to China, if they pass by the "Suyan", it means they are far from Japan and will see the Grand Tang dynasty soon'.[6] As with the earlier text, it has yet to be established whether or not the reference definitively applies to Socotra Rock or another feature (Surhone et al., 2010: 2, 41; "Charting the Diaoyus", 12/10/1996).

Although the feature cannot be found in the early seventeenth-century Selden map, Jeju Island and Japan's Kyushu do appear to be included.[7] However, South Korean organizations such as the Society of Ieodo Research have shed some additional light on the feature's history shortly thereafter. In 2013–14, for example, the group uncovered evidence that suggested the inclusion of the feature in Dutch explorer Hendrik Hamel's (1630–92) navigation charts after he had become shipwrecked on Jeju Island in 1653. Hamel apparently transcribed the feature as *Oost* in Dutch (*East*) in his journal from that period[8] (Chin, 03/02/2014). Historical Korean records acknowledge that other foreign vessels, such as from Russia, carried out surveys in adjacent waters in the 1600s and 1700s. In May 1787, two French fleets surveyed the waters around Ulleungdo in the Sea of Japan.[9] The Japanese also mapped the coastal waters around Korea prior to their colonization of the country in the early 1900s (Koh, 16/11/2011). Evidence exists, which suggests that the Beiyang Fleet (*Northern Seas Fleet* or *Northern Ocean Fleet*), one of late Qing China's four modernized naval fleets, surveyed and documented Socotra Rock from 1880 to 1890 (Guo, 2006: 226). However, it was not until 1900, when the UK merchant ship *Socotra*, en route to Shanghai, China, from the island of Kyushu in Japan, accidentally struck the feature, after which it was given its current internationally recognized name (Chin, 03/02/2014).

According to the United Kingdom Hydrographic Office, a British Royal Navy surveying vessel, the *HMS Waterwitch*, carried out a survey of the rock in August 1901. The survey declared it to be a submerged feature resting 5.5 m (18 feet or 2.95 fathoms) below the water at its highest point. The *Waterwitch*, under Lieutenant Commander W. O. Lyne's command, had searched for the underwater rock reported by the Peninsular and Oriental Company's steamship *Socotra* in 1900 as being northeastward of the Great Yangtze Bank. The *Waterwitch* located it at the coordinates of latitude 32″ 7′ North, longitude 125″ 11′ East, not far from the more precise contemporary coordinates of latitude 32° 07′ 22.63″ North, longitude 125° 10′ 56.81″ East. It was in fact about 8 km southeast of the position given by the *Socotra* in 1900 (United Kingdom Hydrographic Office, 1901).

In 1938, the Japanese, who had formally occupied the Korean Peninsula in 1910, commenced planning for the construction of a substantial artificial structure on the rock, which was to be 15 m in diameter and 35 m above sea level. It was to include a lighthouse and a submarine ferry relay station. The outbreak of the Second World War and more pressing security concerns in the Pacific theater, however, persuaded the Japanese to indefinitely delay these plans. It was not until 1951 that the new post-war Republic of Korea made its first formal attempts to publicize its claim to Ieodo (Korea Hydrographic and Oceanographic Agency, 2010). Such activities were most likely influenced by the fact that the government of US-occupied post-war Japan had been making diplomatic efforts since 1946 to reclaim a number of claimed Korean territories, such as the Liancourt Rocks (Korean, *Dokdo*; Japanese, *Takeshima*) and Ulleungdo Island[10] (Japanese, *Utsuryoshima*). This also took place in a context of tensions and difficult cease-fire talks on the peninsula following the outbreak of the Korean War in June 1950. These activities included a joint survey of the submerged feature by the Korean Navy and, remarkably, the Korean Alpine Mountain Climbing Club in 1951 (Korea Hydrographic and Oceanographic Agency, 2010; Surhone et al., 2010: 2). One of the key participants in the survey was the famous Korean sportsman and writer, Hong Jong-in (Kang Byeong-Cheol, 2012: 214–215). The participants physically planted a copper plate with the engraved words 'Ieodo, Territory of the Republic of Korea' upon the submerged rock (Korea Hydrographic and Oceanographic Agency, 2010; Surhone et al., 2010: 2). As a result of this action at a time when South Korea and China were in conflict during the Korean War, some observers regard 1951 as a starting point for the Socotra Rock dispute (Harress, 02/02/2016). Certainly it was the beginning of a series of long-term political quarreling.

On 19 July 1951, the Republic of Korea's Ambassador to the USA, Yang You Chan, also lobbied the US's Dean Rusk, at that time Assistant Secretary of State for Far Eastern Affairs.[11] Yang wanted the USA to pressure Japan to act in accordance with the Potsdam Declaration of August 1945. This included the unconditional demand that Japan return any territory it had seized over the previous half-century of conquest and colonialism. The Koreans wanted the Japanese government to definitively renounce all titles and claims to the Liancourt Rocks, Parangdo (Ieodo) and any other Korean territories once possessed and claimed by Japan. The South Koreans were particularly eager to secure a commitment from Japan prior to the upcoming termination of the US occupation according to the San Francisco Treaty, which was signed in September 1951 and came into force in April 1952.

While the Liancourt Rocks were and still remain a thorny bilateral issue, Parangdo was not seriously factored into the discussions. Indeed, the US reaction to the Parangdo issue was one of frustration. For example, Yang had asked that the feature be included in the negotiations. John Foster Dulles, who was Consultant to the US Secretary of State Dean Acheson, then enquired about where exactly the features in question were located. Pyo Wook Ham, the First Secretary of the Korean Embassy, responded that they were situated in the East Sea (Sea of Japan) near Ulleungdo. Despite this, the Americans reported that a US State Department expert on international boundaries, Samuel Whittemore Boggs, had 'tried all resources in Washington' at his disposal but was still unable to identify Parangdo. The matter was finally set aside after the ROK withdrew its request to include the rock in the discussions. Rusk controversially rejected the call for Japan to jettison its claims to the Liancourt Rocks and suggested that Parangdo was irrelevant because it was never clearly located and thus perhaps did not exist at all (Rusk Documents, 2012).

In January 1952, the South Koreans unilaterally delineated the controversial Syngman Rhee Peace Line, from which Seoul claimed all territory within it, including Socotra Rock. The purpose of the disputed line was ostensibly to contribute to peace, hence the name, by diplomatically clarifying South Korea's claims and territorial waters. All of South Korea's neighbors, however, including the PRC, refused to recognize the unilaterally drawn line (Surhone et al., 2010: 2). The so-called peace line was in reality a source of friction, particularly between the ROK and Japan. It in fact was eventually superseded in 1965 by the Japan-Korea Fisheries Agreement,[12] although according to Valencia it was never formally withdrawn (Valencia, 2007: 141).

In 1963, a minor spat between the PRC and South Korea developed after the sinking of the Chinese ship *Yuejin*'s maiden voyage between Qingdao (also *Tsingtao*) in northeastern China and Nagoya in Japan. The surviving crew members blamed the incident on a torpedo attack when in reality it had actually struck Socotra Rock. Subsequent investigations found that the main cause of the sinking was a navigational error by the ship's crew. The rock would have been clearly visible on most international navigational and maritime charts at that time. After an extensive search of the area, which began on 1 May, and amid a refusal by Seoul to recognize the activity, the Shanghai Riverside Fleet located the wreck of the *Yuejin* in early June 1963 (Surhone et al., 2010: 2). In 1970, when the South Korean parliament enacted the Maritime Mineral Resource Act, this legally defined the undersea rock as being situated within the state's fourth largest mining field. Beijing protested the legislation and refused to recognize the law's regulations (Surhone et al., 2010: 2).

Relevant to any ultimate demarcation of the Yellow Sea are two demarcation agreements drafted by Japan and South Korea in 1974. These consisted of an agreement involving boundary determination on the adjacent continental shelf and an agreement involving shared development of the continental shelf.[13] Both agreements attempted to address the unresolved issues of overlapping Chinese, Japanese, and South Korean demarcation zones in the northern East China Sea. These were agreements to which the PRC strongly objected, though without stating any specific territorial claim of its own. In response to China's protests, Tokyo and Seoul put off ratification of these agreements until June 1978, when they nonetheless proceeded to ratify them despite Beijing's continued stated disapproval (Drifte, 2008: 5–6).

Prior to the January 1974 draft agreements, ROK negotiators complained that the Japanese Torishima (Dorishima) island group could not reasonably claim a continental shelf area because a deep seabed trench separated it from the Japanese home islands.[14] The South Koreans thus adopted an approach referred to as the 'natural prolongation of the continental shelf principle' to maximize its claims vis-à-vis Japan in that area (Valencia, 2007: 143–144). For their part, the Japanese cited the undisputed ownership of the Danjo Gunto island group to make continental shelf claims. They did this via Article 21 of UNCLOS, arguing the case for a median line demarcation between the said islands and South Korean territory. The ROK maintained the islands were on their own continental shelf. Unable to reach a final agreement and in spite of significant overlap in their respective claim areas, in January 1974, the two neighbors opted instead for a joint jurisdiction solution via a Joint Development Zone (Valencia, 2007: 143–144). It was not until June 1978 that the agreement actually came into effect, doing so with the stipulation that it would remain in place for 50 years. Beyond the 50-year mark of 2028, either state is permitted to end the agreement provided that a three-year notice is given. The PRC claims rights to a significant area of the continental shelf within the Japan-Korean Joint Development Zone (JDZ) (Valencia, 2007: 143–144; 145).

More collaborative efforts were made in the following decade. For example, from 1980 to 1986, Japan and South Korea carried out seven explorations on three sites, but finally abandoned these when it became clear that these fields were not economically viable (Drifte, 2008: 5–6). In 1984, an academic research team from Jeju University and the Korean Broadcasting System's (KBS) Parangdo group conducted a joint investigation of the feature and confirmed its coordinates (Korea Hydrographic and Oceanographic Agency, 2010). In the same year, Seoul decided to commence steps toward the eventual construction of the Ieodo Ocean Research Station (Kang Hyun-kyung, 2012: 214). Two years later, the Korean Office of Hydrographic Affairs (now the Korea Hydrographic and Oceanographic Agency) sent a survey vessel to the area and declared that the feature's depth was 4.6 m (Korea Hydrographic and Oceanographic Agency, 2010). In 1987, the Korean Sea and Harbor Administration formally named the feature 'Ieodo' and attached a floating buoy to it in order to prevent maritime accidents and to assert South Korea's jurisdiction over the surrounding waters (Kang Hyun-kyung, 2012: 215). Five years later, in 1992, the Chinese People's Liberation Army Navy (PLAN) conducted a survey of the rock for the first time ever (Harress, 02/02/2016). It was not until 1995 that the ROK allocated ₩212 billion (US $278 million at 1995 exchange rate) toward the construction of the IORS, which was eventually completed in June 2003 (Kang Hyun-kyung, 2012: 215).

Prior to the 1990s, it is apparent that Socotra Rock was an occasional but very minor irritant in bilateral ties between South Korea and China. Since then, these minor disputes and contradictory positions have hindered the potential for Chinese-Korean cooperation. Despite these and other developments from the 1970s through to the 1990s, Socotra Rock was a persistent irritant, but in the last decade or so has since escalated to a more worrisome level within the wider relationship. Given the fact that fishing and other maritime activities like the construction of artificial facilities on Socotra Rock are central components to this dispute, it is important to explain the contrasting stances adopted by China and South Korea with regards to EEZs and continental shelf rights.

According to Shin Hyon-hee and Song Sang-ho of the Korea Herald, Chinese and South Korean continental shelf claims were a rare example of an intentional and coordinated bilateral effort to counter Japanese ocean floor claims. In May 2012, for example, Japan won international recognition for an expanded and extensive continental shelf area on the basis of the tiny and controversial Okinotorishima atoll. Beijing and Seoul rejected this. Shin and Song argued that the Socotra Rock dispute continued to hinder the full potential for similar PRC-ROK cooperation in countering maritime claims made by Japan (Roehrig, 2012: 70; Park Byong-su, 09/01/2013; Shin Hyon-hee and Song Sang-ho, 10/07/2012). Such claims are noteworthy because they highlight a potential vulnerability in Seoul's negotiating position and the contradictions between its rejection of the natural prolongation approach with China in the Yellow Sea versus its adoption of the same and by now widely rejected approach with regards to Japan in the East China Sea.[15]

Despite this apparent contradiction, Seoul submitted claims in December 2012 to UNCLOS for an extended continental shelf beyond 200 nmi that would extend as far as the Okinawa Trough in the East China Sea. This time, it was Japan and China rejecting the claim. The area coverage was more than twice the continental shelf area estimated in 2009 preliminary documents, which interestingly had been prepared respectively by China and South Korea. The claim took the ROK's continental shelf claims to within 5 nmi of Japan's territorial waters and only 12 nmi from the Okinawan islands. Seoul's claims followed a similar continental claim by Beijing in December 2012. From reviewing these historical highlights, it is easy to see how Socotra Rock was regularly in the spotlight for at least 60 years, and this was at both the popular and political levels. Interest in it rose and fell, and then would rise again, when recent escalations demanded more attention be paid to it.

Summary

This chapter has broadly presented several factors that have weighed heavily on Socotra Rock itself, one of the most important being the continuous historical thread that leads up to the present. However, the historical is just one element out of several that collectively tell its complex story. The interplay of high and low politics and diplomacy, geography, economic zones, natural resources, myth, history, and of course maritime law all need to be considered in order to understand why this has been so difficult to resolve. It is the good intentions and yet the limits of maritime law that demand a closer look in order to know what role it can and cannot play in addressing the conflict.

Notes

1. Koreans usually refer to the Yellow Sea as the West Sea (*Seohae*) and the East China Sea as the South Sea (*Namhae*). The Yellow Sea is understood as being a part of the larger East China Sea. For the purposes of impartiality and convenience, and despite any political implications, this chapter refers to the body of water as the Yellow Sea, its internationally accepted English language name.
2. Haijiao (also Haizhao, Barren Island, Tongdao, Dongdao) not only is 133.3 nmi from Socotra Rock but also has a high-tide elevation 70 nmi off the coast of Shanghai. The ROK rejected it as a PRC base point and in 2008 China began to use Sheshan Dao, 155 nmi from the submerged feature, as a starting point for its claims in the Yellow Sea (Valencia, 2007: 143; Caron and Oral, 2014: 168).
3. This is a term used in international maritime law referring to the complex measuring of the breadth of the territorial sea as officially recognized by coastal states.
4. Interestingly, a December 2013 article in the Chinese government-backed *Global Times* charged that Seoul 'has attempted to confuse public opinion by calling the reef an island and exaggerating the issue as a territorial and sovereignty controversy' (Jian, 18/12/2013).
5. Also, *Lee Chung-joon* or *Yi Chong-jun*.
6. This work can be found within the Laudian Collection of Oxford University's Bodleian Library; see http://www.bodley.ox.ac.uk/users/djh/serica/forNLC/SericaSurvey.pdf.
7. The Selden map has received significant attention since its rediscovery by Robert Batchelor in 2008. See http://seldenmap.bodleian.ox.ac.uk/.
8. Hendrick Hamel, James Burney, Pyŏng-do Yi, 'An Account of the Shipwreck of a Dutch Vessel on the Coast of the Isle of Quelpaert: Together

with the Description of the Kingdom of Corea' (Seoul, Ilchogak, 1954/ Tan'gi 4287).
9. *East Sea* to Koreans.
10. Also, previously known as *Dagelet Island* or *Argonaut Island.*
11. For original documents online, see https://commons.wikimedia.org/wiki/Rusk_documents.
12. For more details on this and other agreements, including Japan-Korea-related treaties from 1950 to 2015, see http://www.ioc.u-tokyo.ac.jp/~worldjpn/documents/indices/JPKR/index-ENG.html.
13. It was specified the agreements were 'concerning the Establishment of Boundary in the Northern Part of the Continental Shelf Adjacent to the two Countries' and 'concerning Joint Development of the Southern Part of the Continental Shelf Adjacent to the two Countries'. See *Documents related to Japan–Korean Peninsula Relations 2016* at http://www.ioc.u-tokyo.ac.jp/~worldjpn/documents/indices/JPKR/index-ENG.html.
14. Referring to the four main islands of Kyushu, Honshu, Shikoku, and Hokkaido.
15. This was also iterated in a December 2013 article in the *Global Times*; see Chao Lü, 'Beijing and Seoul gain much more from close relations'. *Global Times*, 18/12/2013. http://epaper.globaltimes.cn/2013-12-19/41389.htm.

Bibliography

Baek, Hee Youn. "Legend of Ieodo", (14/08/2011), *Jeju Weekly*. http://www.jejuweekly.com/news/articlePrint.html?idxno=1830

Brunet-Jailly, Emmanuel, ed. *Border Disputes: A Global Encyclopedia, Vol. I–III.* Santa Barbara, CA.: ABC-CLIO, 2015.

Cai, Jian. "ADIZ dispute not decisive factor in Sino-Korean ties." *Global Times*, 18/12/2013. http://www.globaltimes.cn/content/832873.shtml

Caron, David D. and Oral Nilufer. *Navigating Straits: Challenges for International Law*. Leiden: Brill, 2014

Charting the Diaoyus' troubled history (12/10/1996), *South China Morning Post*. http://www.scmp.com/article/177627/charting-diaoyus-troubled-history

Chin, Haeng-Nam. "Conflict over the reef's jurisdiction continues to cast a shadow over Korean and Chinese relations." *Jeju Weekly*, 03/02/2014. http://www.jejuweekly.com/news/articleView.html?idxno=3848

Choi, Yearn-hong. 'Ieodo.' *Korea Times*, 25/06/2010. http://www.koreatimes.co.kr/www/news/opinon/2011/04/137_68269.html

Drifte, Reinhard. "From 'Sea of Confrontation' to 'Sea of Peace, Cooperation and Friendship'? – Japan Facing China in the East China Sea," *Japan Aktuell – Journal of Current Japanese Affairs* 16 no. 3 (2008): 27–51.

Guo, Rongxing. Territorial Disputes and Resource Management: A Global Handbook. Hauppauge, New York: Nova Publishers, 2006.

Harress, Christopher. "Chinese Military Aircraft Breach Korean and Japanese Air Defense Zones Near To Disputed Ieodo Island." *International Business Times*, 02/02/2016. http://www.ibtimes.com/chinese-military-aircraft-breach-korean-japanese-air-defense-zones-near-disputed-2290227

Kang, Byeong-Cheol. "Ieodo, Okinotorishima and International Politics," Society of Ieodo Research (2012).

Kang, Hyun-kyung. "Ieodo protector sparks imagination of Jeju islanders." *Korea Times*, 12/10/2010. http://www.koreatimes.co.kr/www/news/nation/2016/06/113_77786.html

Kang, Hyun-kyung. "KIPA's new book tackles Dokdo, Ieodo sovereignty." *Korea Times*, 11/10/2012. http://www.koreatimes.co.kr/www/news/nation/2012/10/116_122033.html

Kim, Young-jin. "Why Ieodo matters." *Korea Times*, 18/09/2012. http://www.koreatimes.co.kr/www/news/nation/2012/09/117_120266.html

Koh, Choong-suk. "New boat plying from Jeju to Ieodo." *Korea Times*, 16/11/2011. http://www.koreatimes.co.kr/www/news/opinon/2012/02/198_98884.html

Korea Hydrographic and Oceanographic Agency. "Ieodo." 2010. http://eng.khoa.go.kr/kcom/cnt/selectContentsPage.do?cntId=ieodo_submain

Park, Byong-su. "South Korea claims larger continental shelf." *Hankyoreh*, 09/01/2013. http://english.hani.co.kr/arti/english_edition/e_international/568898.html

Roehrig, Terence. "Republic of Korea Navy and China's Rise: Balancing Competing Priorities." In *CNA Maritime Asia Project Workshop Two: Naval Developments in Asia*, edited by Michael A. McDevitt and Catherine K. Lea, 61–78. Alexandria, Va.: Center for Naval Analyses, 2012.

Rusk Documents. 2012. https://commons.wikimedia.org/wiki/Rusk_documents

Shin, Hae-in. "China demanded S. Korea stop activities near Ieodo." *Korea Herald*, 27/07/2011. http://www.koreaherald.com/national/Detail.jsp?newsMLId=20110727000696

Shin, Hyon-hee and Song Sang-ho. "Korea, China, Japan in race over continental shelves." *Korea Herald*, 10/07/2012. http://www.koreaherald.com/view.php?ud=20120710001337

Song, Sang-ho. "Ieodo not part of territorial dispute with China: Lee." *Korea Herald*, 12/03/2012. http://www.koreaherald.com/national/Detail.jsp?newsMLId=20120312001239

Song, Sang-il. "Ieodo, A Growing Legend." Ieodo Journal 2, (2012).

Su Yan jiao (13/03/2012), *China.com.cn*. http://www.china.com.cn/guoqing/2012-03/13/content_24882839.htm

Surhone, Lambert M., Mariam T. Tennoe and Susan F. Henssonow, eds. *Socotra Rock – Reef, Territorial Dispute, Exclusive Economic Zone, Marado, Jeju-do.* Beau Bassin, Mauritius: VDM Publishing, 2010.

Valencia, Mark J. "The East China Sea Dispute: Context, Claims, Issues, and Possible Solutions," *Asian Perspective* 31, no. 1 (2007): 127–167.

Van Dyke, Jon M. "Ieodo." *Maritime Boundary Disputes in the East China Sea* (conference), Seoul, South Korea, 30/06/2011–01/07/2011.

CHAPTER 2

The Limits of Maritime Law

Abstract This chapter explains the central components to the contrasting legal stances adopted by China and South Korea with regards to Exclusive Economic Zones (EEZs) and continental shelf rights. Because maritime law is often referred to by both parties, certain basics of maritime law need to be understood when examining this topic. Their claims include China's natural prolongation of 'its' continental shelf and South Korea's more internationally accepted median line solution with the submerged feature located well within Seoul's EEZ. These claims overlap, and Socotra Rock rests within the overlapping area. The crux of the dispute is thus not territorial, but rather one concerning the right to exercise jurisdictional authority while also protecting against 'foreign' intervention. These also tie directly into national and regional security concerns, making it important to clarify where international legal practice tends to stand on these questions of equidistance, proportionality, natural prolongation, jurisdiction, and freedom of navigation.

Keywords Maritime law • Exclusive Economic Zones (EEZs) • Continental shelf rights

Because maritime law is so central to this dispute, a fundamental understanding of maritime law needs to be considered when examining it. This includes explaining the key components of the contrasting legal stances adopted by China and South Korea with regards to their respective

S. Fox, *China, South Korea, and the Socotra Rock Dispute*,
https://doi.org/10.1007/978-981-13-2077-4_2

Exclusive Economic Zones (EEZs) and continental shelf rights. Their claims include China's natural prolongation of its continental shelf and South Korea's more internationally accepted median line solution with the submerged feature located well within Seoul's EEZ. These claims overlap, and Socotra Rock rests within the overlapping area. It was mentioned earlier that the crux of the dispute is thus not territorial, but instead concerns the right to exercise jurisdictional authority while also protecting against foreign intervention. These also tie directly into national and regional security concerns, making it important to clarify where international legal practice tends to stand on these questions of equidistance, proportionality, natural prolongation, jurisdiction, and freedom of navigation.

This inevitably touches directly on some pressing questions as to how a rising China interprets internationally accepted maritime laws, and explains why the overriding informed opinion is that China's natural prolongation stance is weak. From here, this leads to reasoning in regard to the Chinese belief that no activities should take place short of a final resolution. In addition, why Beijing argues that a permanent demarcation should be based on 'equitable geographical representation' is also fully laid out. Indeed, legal scholars claim that both states are in breach of the letter and spirit of maritime law, although the two sides are unlikely to seek recourse in international arbitration.[1] In spite of this, the two countries often try, with occasional difficulty, to avoid an escalation of tensions over the feature by agreeing to disagree. This attempt to avoid escalation has taken place in spite of a rise in the number of confrontational activities since South Korea constructed the Ieodo Ocean Research Station in 2003.

UNCLOS

The United Nations Convention on the Law of the Sea (UNCLOS) concluded in 1982 and was intended to replace several other earlier treaties (UNCLOS, 1994). It was to be another 12 years before it actually entered into force in 1994, and its purpose was not only to lay out the maritime rights and responsibilities of states, though this was of course a primary objective. It also concerned commercial activity as well as the environment, the latter including the conservation and use of natural resources. Conflicting legal interpretations of UNCLOS are at the core of this and similar maritime disputes involving China.

There are two principles in conflict with each other here, one based on the natural prolongation of the continental shelf and the other involving a median or equidistant line being decided on in disputed territory. Briefly put, because the specific distance between Korea and China in this case is less than the standard 200 nmi limit allowed for a state's EEZ, this means their respective zones overlap.[2] When similar cases have been brought before the International Court of Justice (ICJ) and arbitral tribunals in the recent past, the more internationally accepted equidistant median line approach has been applied.

It was on the basis of such recent legal trends and decisions that Seoul unilaterally assumed the equidistant principle to address the dispute. This middle line method of demarcation thus locates Socotra Rock well within the ROK's EEZ. It also means that South Korea is entitled under UNCLOS to exercise the rights and privileges of the coastal owner state within the said area. This, however, was rejected by Beijing and is discussed subsequently. This is despite the fact that Ieodo is situated almost exactly in the middle of the overlapping area between China's perceived EEZ and continental shelf boundary and the ROK's median line (see Map 2.1).

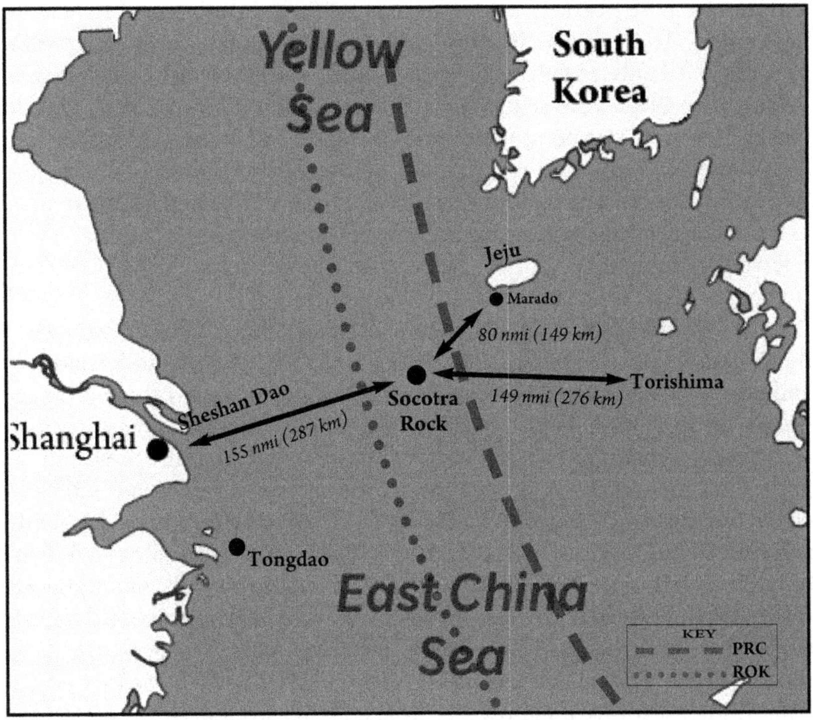

Map 2.1 Socotra Rock is located almost exactly between China's claimed EEZ boundary and the ROK's EEZ boundary. The feature's approximate distances from the nearest islands are also shown

It is important to bear in mind that the feature is permanently below water at both high and low tide. As such, and under Article 121 of UNCLOS, it is not entitled to any maritime zone around it and has no related EEZ, continental shelf zone, or territorial sea area. The Ieodo Ocean Research Station and any other unnatural structure built upon the rock would fall under the convention's Article 60(8), which regards such constructions to be artificial. Article 60 places Ieodo's current above-sea weather station in the category of an artificial island, and thus it is not permitted to demarcate any maritime zone around it. Paragraphs (4) and (5) of this same article do allow for an exception to demarcation, which permits a safety zone maximum of 500 meters.

The relevant section (b) of Article 60 (1) declares that inside the EEZ, the coastal state has 'the exclusive right to construct and to authorize and regulate the construction, operation, and use of … installations and structures for the purposes provided for in Article 56 and other economic purposes'. This also applies to 'installations and structures, which may interfere with the exercise of the rights of the coastal State in the zone'. Article 80 then reflects back on Article 60, stating that this 'applies *mutatis mutandis* to artificial islands, installations and structures on the continental shelf'.[3] Because the PRC sees itself as the rightful coastal state, it views the Ieodo Ocean Research Station as illegal and interfering with the exercise of their own sovereign rights and jurisdiction. Article 74, in relation to EEZs, and Article 83, concerning continental shelves, stipulates that maritime demarcations 'shall be effected by agreement on the basis of international law as referred to in Article 38[4] of the Statute of the International Court of Justice, in order to achieve an equitable solution'.

Importantly, Article 74(3) points out that when there is no agreed demarcation line, competing claimants should 'in a spirit of understanding and co-operation … make every effort to enter into provisional arrangements of a practical nature and, during this transitional period, not to jeopardize or hamper the reaching of the final agreement'. Some might argue that the unilateral actions conducted by South Korea and China in contested areas such as around Socotra Rock could be interpreted as being inconsistent with not only Article 74(3)'s 'spirit of understanding and co-operation' but three additional UNCLOS articles as well, among them 83(3), 300, and 301. In fact, Articles 300 and 301 emphasize, respectively, that parties should act in good faith and 'exercise the rights, jurisdiction and freedoms recognized in this Convention in a manner which would not constitute an abuse of right' and 'shall refrain from any threat or use of force against the territorial integrity or political independence of any State'. China and South Korea's contrasting demarcation claims pick up on these last points, and are discussed subsequently.

Prolongation Versus the Median Line

Both parties believe that it is themselves who have rights and privileges on and around the submerged feature, and this explains the frequent protests and activities aimed at displaying claims. More precisely, if a state lays claim to an EEZ, then UNCLOS Article 1(a) stipulates:

> *the Coastal state has sovereign rights for the purpose of exploring and exploiting, conserving and managing the natural resources, whether living or non-living, of the waters superjacent to the seabed and its subsoil, and with regard to other activities for the economic exploitation and exploration of the zone, such as the production of energy from the water, currents and wind.*

Both the PRC and the ROK assert that Socotra Rock sits on their own respective continental shelves and cite UNCLOS regulations concerning related rights to defend their positions. Article 76 (1), for example, outlines this more precisely when it states:

> the continental shelf of a coastal State comprises the seabed and subsoil of the submarine areas that extend beyond its territorial sea throughout the natural prolongation of its land territory to the outer edge of the continental margin, or to a distance of 200 nautical miles from the baselines from which the breadth of the territorial sea is measured where the outer edge of the continental margin does not extend up to that distance.

Sovereignty rights over a vast continental shelf permit the coastal state to explore and exploit its natural resources, such as mineral and other non-living resources of the seabed. Article 77(2) denies to any other state the ability to undertake any such activities without the coastal state's express consent. The guidelines in Article 76(8) also stipulate that coastal states laying claim to a continental shelf area must submit their claims and demarcations vis-à-vis the limits of the continental shelf beyond 200 nmi to the Commission on the Limits of the Continental Shelf (CLCS) under Annex II and 'on the basis of equitable geographical representation'. This call for equitable geographical representation, which considers the length of the PRC's coastline, the PRC's population, as well as its larger economy, is arguably a major explanatory factor, though not the only one, in Beijing's defense of its natural prolongation of the continental shelf versus median line claims. Chinese scholars also often cite the 1985 continental shelf case involving Libya and Malta as an example of a revised demarcation line, which reflects a more equitable solution (Pan, 2009: 157–159).

In both their East China Sea and Yellow Sea claims, the PRC holds that the natural prolongation stance should apply. This would see China claiming jurisdictional rights over a large portion of the continental shelf area off its coast as far as a 'silt line', which is derived from the maximum distance traveled by sediments that later blanket the seabed. The silt line in this case originates from the Huang He (also Hwang Ho), meaning 'Yellow River' and from which the Yellow Sea derives its name, and the Yangtze River in China. This amounts to the Chinese claiming approximately two-thirds of the Yellow Sea (Zastrow, *Nature*, 15/12/2015). Park discussed this dilemma as far back as 1981, before the completion of UNCLOS, where he pointed out even then that 'none of them is prepared to compromise its claims'. He also noted how 'delimitation of the continental shelf by South Korea is based on the median-line principle toward China in the Yellow Sea and the natural prolongation of land territory principle toward Japan in the East China Sea', perhaps revealing at that time a convenient flexibility toward the two principles (Choon-Ho Park, 1981: 452, 447). Presently the silt line extends well beyond the ROK's median line, the latter being widely accepted as the appropriate method of demarcation. China's claim, if accepted, would see it controlling an even larger area than before, including most of the Japanese-Korean Joint Development Zone, which China does not recognize (Van Dyke, 2003: 29).

Van Dyke has examined this closely, and has further pointed out that the median line approach, also referred to as the equidistant approach, has been utilized as an aid to resolution, but it is not binding nor mandatory. This reality was seen in the 1985 Libya/Malta case, the 1984 Gulf of Maine case, and the 1993 Jan Mayen case,[5] where the original equidistant line was readjusted after examination by the ICJ in order to factor in considerations such as the length and proportionality of coastlines to increase the chances of a final demarcation being 'equitable' (Van Dyke, 2003: 3). It is additionally noted that despite these exceptional cases, the international legal track record also points to the fact that non-geographical factors such as 'fisheries, ecological data and the economic needs of coastal communities' will rarely have any bearing on a delimitation decision and that geographical factors tend to be the overriding influence. He adds that the natural prolongation approach, although a geographical factor, is an outdated mode of demarcation that has been rendered obsolete since the early 1980s (Van Dyke, 2003: 4–5). Writing in 2003, he indicated that consideration for the vital security interests of each party had been a characteristic of all recent decisions where tribunals have opted against an all-or-nothing solution in favor of resolutions that were sensitive to the vital security interests of the respective parties (Van Dyke, 2003: 10–11).

According to these trends, he concluded that tribunals

> tend to give each competing country some of what they seek, to protect their vital security interests, and, to some extent, to split the difference between the countries in order to achieve the 'equitable solution' sought by Articles 74 and 83 of the Law of the Sea Convention. Another important emerging trend is that most countries now prefer a single maritime boundary that divides the exclusive economic zone and the continental shelf at the same location. The factors governing these two separate delimitations are the same, and it is convenient in most regions to have the same line for both boundaries. (Van Dyke, 2003: 11–12)

Given the changes in context over the past 15 years, the likelihood of China and South Korea agreeing to international arbitration is unlikely. One observer interprets China's strategy as an effort to demarcate the overlapping EEZ area on the basis of equity after a series of long negotiations. This interpretation sees similarities with how China resolved its Gulf of Tonkin (Beibu Bay)[6] dispute with Vietnam in 2004. This resolution witnessed China conceding more to Vietnam (at a ratio of 1.5–1) on the basis of Vietnam's longer coastline. The Chinese have already signed two agreements with the Vietnamese, effective from 2004, regarding the management of fisheries and boundary delimitation in the Gulf of Tonkin (Kang Hyun-kyung, 2012: 217). As its first maritime boundary agreement, the Chinese point to the Gulf of Tonkin agreement with Vietnam, with which it has other maritime disagreements, as a satisfactory solution to bilateral disputes (Amer and Li, 29/05/2015).

Parallels between the Gulf of Tonkin and Yellow Sea cases are, however, difficult to draw. For one reason, as observed by Lee, even though UNCLOS guidelines include an equitable principle, the idea of an equitable outcome regarding the Yellow Sea and a part of the East China Sea appears to be unrealistic and elusive. This is most clearly indicated by the fact that there were 14 rounds of inconclusive negotiations between 1996 and 2008, and these negotiations only resumed again in 2015 after a hiatus of 7 years. An additional complicating factor is the effect of any Sino-South Korean line on maritime talks between China and North Korea, who have not yet agreed on their own respective maritime zones in the northern Yellow Sea, although North Korea appears to agree with the median line principle. To date, Beijing and Pyongyang have only concluded one maritime agreement, that is the China-North Korea Joint Offshore Petroleum Development Agreement in 2005 (Lee Jae-min, 29/12/2015).[7]

Arguments Against Prolongation

The prevailing opinion among leading international maritime law experts is that China's natural prolongation of the continental shelf stance is weak, though this does not prevent China from often citing the ICJ's 1969 finding in the North Sea Continental Shelf Cases between Germany, the Netherlands, and Denmark in an attempt to bolster its stance despite the notable differences between the cases. In the 1969 case, the Netherlands and Denmark proposed that the continental shelf should be delineated according to equidistant lines, though with adjustments if 'special circumstances' were factored in. This was rejected in favor of a finding, which declared that the area of the continental shelf constitutes a natural prolongation of each state's land territory into and under the sea. The summary of the judgment states, 'the Court found in each case that the use of the equidistance method of delimitation was not obligatory … that delimitation was to be effected by agreement in accordance with equitable principles and taking account of all relevant circumstances', and among the factors that should be considered was 'the element of a reasonable degree of proportionality between the extend of the continental shelf areas appertaining to each State and the length of its coast' (International Court of Justice, 1969).[8]

However, since the 1970s and the negotiations which led to UNCLOS in 1982 with its emphasis on EEZs, the natural prolongation stance has witnessed a marked decline in support and has even been referred to as debatable. The unique circumstances of the continental shelf in the North Sea case were crucial to the ultimate reasoning behind the judgment but this is unlikely to recur, thus making a reliance on such geological factors ultimately problematic and possibly irrelevant.[9] The ever-changing contexts of contemporary international relations also challenges the idea of decisions based purely on an unchanging geography. Rather, a push or trend developed where there were not to be any perceived winners or losers, but instead beneficiaries of an equitable solution for all the parties involved. The acceptance and eventual ratification of UNCLOS after the 1970s has also seen natural prolongation arguments being turned down in favor of findings which granted little or no attention to the topography of the seabed, but instead permitted states to claim an EEZ and continental shelf which can be extended to 200 nmi. In cases such as between South Korea and China in the Yellow Sea and the northern East China Sea, UNCLOS Article 76 discourages continental shelf geomorphic considerations when judging the delimitation of the continental shelf between states with opposite or adjacent coasts.

Considering how cases have been decided with UNCLOS as the internationally accepted guideline for maritime disputes, it is likely that the PRC's arguments concerning the continental shelf and silt lines would be relatively weak if presented before an international tribunal. Even within China, there is a growing consensus among legal experts that in cases such as these, the equidistance solution rather than natural prolongation is the most practical route to agreement and is now accepted as a standard in customary international law. It has been noted in a sample survey of 134 bilateral maritime delimitation agreements from 1940 to 1993, for example, 103 of these were addressed in one way or another via the equidistant principle method (Legault & Hankey, 1993: 214).

Another factor which appears to undermine Beijing's stance is how the topography of the Yellow Sea is such that a natural prolongation stance cannot be reasonably applied because the sea's floor is shallow, flat, and relatively featureless throughout. China's Yellow Sea claims are in marked contrast to its claims in the East China Sea, where the seabed declines at a slight angle as it moves away from the Chinese coast before descending abruptly at the deep Okinawan Trough lying west of Japan's southernmost islands. The seabed sediments of the Yellow Sea also do not change abruptly from clay to sand but rather make a gradual and smooth transition and include areas where the sediments mix (Van Dyke, 2011: 14).[10]

A number of leading Chinese scholars have likewise been casting doubt on the applicability today of the natural prolongation approach, even as far back as 2000. Zou Keyuan, for example, stated in 2000 that the PRC had recently started to realize, given the general acceptance of the equidistant principle, the difficulties attached to applying the natural prolongation principle in its maritime disputes. Rather, it began to examine the advantages for China of a principle of delimitation based on proportionality. He did add, however, that China might still insist on a natural prolongation principle when demarcating its continental shelf (Zou, 2000: 77–78).

Ji Guoxing has also concurred regarding how controversial the continental shelf approach has been, and that definitions in maritime law are in the midst of an evolutionary process which has tended to complicate rather than clarify. Pointing out that 'the doctrine of natural prolongation has been overridden by the 200 nmi limit regime', he adds that this has led to the former's loss of credibility[11] (Ji, 1995: 18). The continental shelf approach has additionally been pointedly critiqued by yet another scholar, Jonathan I. Charney, whose comment in 1994 still holds true today:

> international forums have been unable to delimit maritime boundaries on the basis of geologic considerations because of the uncertainties of that science, the difficulty of adapting it to international maritime boundaries that require relatively precise delimitation, and the minimal relevance of such considerations to contemporary international relations. (Charney, 1994: 239)

Given such generally accepted views, it seems South Korea will not feel pressured to concede to China's position in the Yellow Sea. At the same time, while the PRC's prolongation and proportionality stance is difficult to defend at the broader level, there may be hope in Beijing that, as with the 2004 Gulf of Tonkin agreement with Vietnam as well as Seoul's natural prolongation position vis-à-vis Japan in the northern East China Sea, that South Korea might be willing to agree to revised demarcations in the interest of Sino-South Korean ties more generally. For now, the fact that Socotra Rock is closer to Korean territory than any other state's territory, has a South Korean research station upon it, and has a long history of Korean activities on the rock, all serve to buttress Seoul's arguments that the submerged rock lies within South Korea's EEZ and that South Korea has more robust rights to it ("Ieodo seminar explores Korea's", 30/06/2011).

Security Factors and Other Considerations

In addition to this dispute being an issue concerning the rights of one country to act, to administer, and to extract potentially valuable resources within its perceived EEZ and on its perceived continental shelf, it is also about protecting these rights against 'foreign' intervention. This directly ties into national security concerns because the Chinese have long been accused of unfairly claiming that UNCLOS provisions permit them to forbid military activities within 'their' EEZ. This has been evidenced in confrontations with US naval vessels in the South China Sea in 2009 (Fisher, 2009). The PRC has also suspected that the EEZ assertions of such rival claimants as Japan, for example, reveal a 'shielded motive', where the act of ostensibly defending one state's EEZ is in reality a type of sea denial aimed at containing the PRC and its naval vessels (Hsiung, 2007: 144). The PRC's position on its purported EEZ area is that all non-Chinese military vessels must provide the Chinese authorities prior notice before entering what they consider to be China's EEZ. It also holds that activities such as intelligence gathering, hydrography, and surveying by foreign vessels are illegal. However, as argued by Kang, 'To be consistent with its demand that the U.S. cease performing military operations, China would not be able to undertake any military operations in the waters of South Korea's EEZ' (Kang Byeong-Cheol, 2013: 113). It has also been noted that 'As such, to preserve its own security interests, China prefers a status quo policy and used strategic ambiguity on the Ieodo issue' (Kim Young-jin, 18/09/2012). UNCLOS Article 58 (1), for example, stresses that in the EEZ, all member states enjoy 'the freedoms referred to in Article 87 of navigation and overflight and of the laying of submarine cables and pipelines, and other internationally lawful uses of the sea related to these freedoms'. While UNCLOS appears non-committal about directly addressing maritime military activities, the US government made clear its position when stating in 1982 (at the conclusion of UNCLOS III—from 1973 to 1982) that 'military operations, exercises and activities have always been regarded as internationally lawful uses of the sea' and that 'the right to conduct such activities will continue to be enjoyed by all States in the exclusive economic zone'.

Beijing rejects Seoul's position not only on the basis of the natural prolongation of the continental shelf as they see it, but also on the basis of the historical record (Zhao Quansheng, 2011: 147). Under this argument, it is the PRC and not South Korea who should have ultimate authority in terms of EEZ rights and privileges on and around Socotra Rock. At the very least, the submerged rock is located within a still unresolved and overlapping EEZ area. As such, in the interests of peaceful relations, no state should act unilaterally without the consultation of the other. In accordance with how Beijing interprets UNCLOS, South Korean activities within the overlapping area and on Socotra Rock are a breach of China's EEZ rights, and must be continuously protested against (Flenniken, 14/08/2011). As mentioned earlier, the Chinese also argue that any final bilaterally agreed delimitation should take place based on a sense of fairness which factors in a longer coastline and a larger population and economy for the PRC (Jung, 08/08/2008). Beijing's stance is also influenced by views which declare that the seabeds of peripheral waters have been formed over thousands of years by mineral-rich sediments which have flowed down from China's rivers into such areas as the Yellow Sea and the East China Sea (Cohen and Van Dyke, 26/10/2010).

Agreeing to Disagree

Despite these disagreements, both countries have sought to calm tensions or misunderstandings over the feature by emphasizing that the issue centers on EEZs and not on the more sensitive question of physical territory or the sovereignty of a land feature. Both have agreed that, in accordance with UNCLOS regulations, the rock cannot be legally claimed as the actual territory of any one state ("China demands South Korea stop", 27/07/2011). Senior ROK and PRC politicians have repeatedly stated that the Socotra Rock issue is not a territorial dispute, and this was emphasized, for example, by South Korean President Lee Myung-bak in March 2012 that the dispute was more an issue of maritime delimitation. This statement followed an angry South Korean reaction to remarks made by Liu Cigui, director of China's State Oceanic Administration (SOA) on 3 March 2012 in which he asserted Chinese rights to the area (Kang Hyun-kyung, 12/03/2012).

Since the construction of the IORS in June 2003, the PRC's Foreign Affairs Ministry has frequently declared that the two states have no territorial dispute over Socotra Rock. However, the Ministry has also stated that any unilateral activities by the South Koreans have no legal effect on the feature's status. Following the PRC's controversial Air Defense Identification Zone (ADIZ) declaration on 23 November 2013, PRC Foreign Ministry spokesperson Qin Gang once more declared that it had 'no territorial dispute' with South Korea regarding the feature, that the two countries are 'friendly neighbors', that China hoped to resolve the issue through 'friendly consultations and negotiations' and expressed hope 'that we can win coordination and understanding from the ROK side' (Kim Ji-hyun, 25/11/2013).[12] The Korean Herald has also reported that the two governments understand Socotra Rock cannot be claimed by either side and is thus not a disputed territory. South Korea's Foreign Ministry has also publicly confirmed this. Both states have also agreed not to dispute the ownership of the submerged rock (Shin Hae-in, 27/07/2011). It is apparent, however, that while Socotra Rock cannot legally impact on the extent of either state's EEZ, South Korean activities do strengthen Seoul's median line position and weaken Beijing's natural prolongation stance on the basis of its physical, active, and continuous display of authority in the area. It also seems remarkable for Seoul to have invested a substantial amount of time and money since the late 1990s and early 2000s to buttress its presence on the rock for the strict purposes of predicting the weather and other scientific endeavors. Thus, while international law does not permit South Korea to claim actual ownership of Ieodo, its developments on the feature leave people in no doubt as to who holds the strongest position on the issue. Under UNCLOS, EEZ rights and privileges also permit a coastal state to build artificial structures within its designated EEZ waters, and South Korean activities on Socotra Rock are a very public display and exercise of this right. A rise in the number of actions since 2003 aimed at strengthening and countering conflicting claims lies at the heart of fluctuating and heightening bilateral tensions.

Notes

1. For an overview, see Kim Suk Kyoon (2017), 'Maritime Boundary Negotiations between China and Korea: The Factors at Stake', *The International Journal of Marine and Coastal Law*, 32, no. 1: 69–94.
2. Precisely where to begin to measure either EEZ or territorial limits from is another legal complication. These 'baseline' points are discussed at length in legal literature; see, for example: Robert Beckman, 'The UN Convention on the Law of the Sea and the Maritime Disputes in the South China Sea', *American Journal of International Law* 107, no. 1 (January 2013): 142–163; Clive Schofield, 'Challenges in Defining the "boundary" between land and sea', National University of Singapore Centre for International Law Roundtable on the South China Sea, *International Law and UNCLOS,* 27–28 June 2013, https://cil.nus.edu.sg/wp-content/uploads/2013/04/Session-2-Schofield-Baselines-Issues-in-the-South-China-Sea.pdf; Stuart B. Kaye, 'Territorial Sea Baselines along Ice-Covered Coasts: International Practice and Limits of the Law of the Sea', *Ocean Development & International Law* 35, Issue 1 (2004): 75–102; Farhad Talaie, 'The Issue of Straight Baselines in the International Law of the Sea and State Practice', *Maritime Studies* 1999, Issue 105 (1999): 5–21.

3. The term mutatis mutandis is defined as 'the necessary changes. This is a phrase of frequent practical occurrence, meaning that matters or things are generally the same, but to be altered, when necessary, as to names, office, and the like.' https://legal-dictionary.thefreedictionary.com/Mutatis+mutandis.
4. For more, see http://www.icj-cij.org/documents/?p1=4&p2=2#CHAPTER_II.
5. For more on the latter two cases, see http://www.icj-cij.org/docket/index.php?sum=401&p1=3&p2=3&case=78&p3=5.
6. For example, see http://www.chinausfocus.com/peace-security/maritime-delimitation-in-the-gulf-of-tonkin-is-too-important-to-be-ignored/.
7. For more on North Korea's exploration and delimitation-related activities in the Yellow Sea, see http://38north.org/wp-content/uploads/2015/12/Bermudez-NK-Exploration-Oil-Gas.pdf.
8. For the entire case, see http://www.icj-cij.org/files/case-related/51/051-19690220-JUD-01-00-EN.pdf.
9. Wolfgang Friedmann, 'The North Sea Continental Shelf Cases—A Critique', *American Journal of International Law* 64, no. 2 (April 1970), 229–240.
10. For a fuller discussion of the North Sea cases and related issues, see, for example, Shuqing Qiao et al., 'Sediment accumulation and budget in the Bohai Sea, Yellow Sea and East China Sea', *Marine Geology* 390, no.1 (August 2017), 270–281; Jianwei Wei, et al., 'Clay mineral distributions in the southern Yellow Sea and their significance', *Chinese Science Bulletin* 48, Suppl 1 (June 2003): 7–11; Herman A. Karl, 'Sediments of the Sea Floor' at https://pubs.usgs.gov/circ/c1198/chapters/090-100_Sediment.pdf.
11. He additionally refers here to two sources to make this point: David Joseph Attard, *The Exclusive Economic Zone in International Law*, Oxford University Press, 1987; and Douglas M. Johnston and Mark J. Valencia, *Pacific Ocean Boundary Problems, Status and Solutions*, Netherlands: Springer, 1991.
12. According to Kang, during PRC President Hu Jintao's state visit to South Korea on 25 August 2008, references to 'Suyan Rock' were intentionally removed from official PRC websites. Hu also called for the two sides to engage in peaceful dialogue and negotiations toward resolving their overlapping EEZs (Kang Hyun-kyung, 2012: 219).

Bibliography

Amer, Ramses and Li Jianwei. "Maritime Delimitation in the Gulf of Tonkin is Too Important to be Ignored." *ChinaUSFocus*, 29/05/2015. http://www.chinausfocus.com/peace-security/maritime-delimitation-in-the-gulf-of-tonkin-is-too-important-to-be-ignored/

Charney, Jonathan I. "Progress in International Maritime Boundary Delimitation Law," *American Journal of International Law* 88, no. 2 (1994): 227–256.

China demands S. Korea stop hoisting sunken ship near Ieodo (27/07/2011), *Yonhap News Agency.* http://english.yonhapnews.co.kr/national/2011/07/27/19/0301000000AEN20110727006300315F.html

Cohen, Jerome A. and Jon M. Van Dyke. "Finding its Sea Legs." South China Morning Post, 26/10/2010. https://www.scmp.com/article/728520/finding-its-sea-legs

Fisher, Richard Jr. "South China Sea Competition: China Contemplates More Mischief," *International Assessment and Strategy Center*, 28/06/ 2009. http://www.strategycenter.net/research/pubID.209/pub_detail.asp

Flenniken, Lauren. "Claiming Ieodo Rock: Maritime boundary disputes remain deadlocked between South Korea and China." *Jeju Weekly*, 14/08/2011. http://www.jejuweekly.com/news/articleView.html?idxno=1829

Hsiung, James C. "Sea Power, Law of the Sea, and a Sino-Japanese East China Sea 'Resource War.'" In *China and Japan at Odds: Deciphering the Perpetual Conflict*, edited by James C. Hsiung, 133–154. New York: Palgrave Macmillan, 2007.

International Court of Justice. "North Sea Continental Shelf Cases: Denmark/Federal Judgement of 20 February 1969". http://www.icj-cij.org/files/case-related/5L1/5537.pdf

Ji, Guoxing. "Maritime Jurisdiction in The Three China Seas: Options for Equitable Settlement." *Institute on Global Conflict and Cooperation*, Policy Paper 19 (1995). https://escholarship.org/uc/item/7rq2b069

Jung, Sung-ki. "S. Korea to Ask China to Rectify Claim Over Ieodo." *Korea Times*, 08/08/2008. http://www.koreatimes.co.kr/www/news/nation/2011/04/205_29027.html

Kang, Byeong-Cheol. "Ieodo, Okinotorishima and International Politics," *Journal of Peace Studies* 14, no.2 (2013): 99–118. http://koreajoongangdaily.joins.com/news/article/article.aspx?aid=2981469

Kang, Hyun-kyung. "Lee says Ieodo not territorial dispute." *Korea Times*, 12/03/2012. http://www.koreatimes.co.kr/www/news/nation/2012/03/116_106794.html

Kim, Ji-hyun. "China informed Seoul of air defense zone." *Korea Herald*, 25/11/2013. http://www.koreaherald.com/view.php?ud=20131125001000

Kim, Se-jeong. "Ieodo seminar explores Korea's new frontier." *Korea Times*, 30/06/2011. http://www.koreatimes.co.kr/www/news/nation/2012/02/359_89975.html

Kim, Young-jin. "Why Ieodo matters." *Korea Times*, 18/09/2012. http://www.koreatimes.co.kr/www/news/nation/2012/09/117_120266.html

Lee, Jae-min. "Equitable share of maritime zone." *Korea Herald*, 29/12/2015. http://www.koreaherald.com/view.php?ud=20151229001062

Legault, Leonard and Blair Hankey. (1993) "Method, Oppositeness and Adjacency, and Proportionality in Maritime Boundary Delimitation," 203–242 in Charney, J.I. and Alexander, L.M. (eds.) *International Maritime Boundaries*, Vol. I, Dordrecht: Martinus Nijhoff. (1996).

Pan, Junwu. *Toward a New Framework for Peaceful Settlement of China's Territorial and Boundary Disputes*. Leiden: Martinus Nijhoff Publishers, 2009.

Park, Choon-Ho. "Maritime Claims in the China Seas: Current State Practices," *San Diego Law Review* 18, no. 3 (April 1981): 443–454.

Shin, Hae-in. "China demanded S. Korea stop activities near Ieodo." *Korea Herald*, 27/07/2011. http://www.koreaherald.com/national/Detail.jsp?newsMLId=20110727000696

United Nations Convention on the Law of the Sea, Montego Bay, Jamaica, 16 November 1994, *United Nations Treaty Series*, vol. 1833. http://www.un.org/depts/los/convention_agreements/texts/unclos/unclos_e.pdf

Van Dyke, Jon M. "The Republic of Korea's Maritime Boundaries," Honolulu, Hawaii: *William S. Richardson School of Law*, University of Hawaii at Manoa, 2003. http://webcache.googleusercontent.com/search?q=cache:F8E1lcIosdsJ:www.hawaii.edu/elp/publications/faculty/TheRepublicofKorea.doc+&cd=1&hl=ja&ct=clnk&gl=jp

Van Dyke, Jon M. "Ieodo." *Maritime Boundary Disputes in the East China Sea* (conference), Seoul, South Korea, 30/06/2011–01/07/2011.

Zastrow, Mark. "Yellow Sea talks raise hopes for marine science," *Nature* 528 (15 December 2015). http://www.nature.com/news/yellow-sea-talks-raise-hopes-for-marine-science 1.19027

Zhao, Quansheng. "China's Northeast Water Frontiers, East China Sea Disputes and Co-Management Approach." In: Hao, Yufan, and Bill K. P. Chou (eds.), *China's Policies on its Borderlands and the International Implications*. Singapore: World Scientific Publishing, 2011.

Zou, Keyuan. "China's Exclusive Economic Zones and Continental Shelf: Developments, Problems, and Prospects," *Marine Policy* 25, no. 1 (2000): 71–81.

CHAPTER 3

Bilateral Challenges and Korean Anxieties

Abstract This chapter examines the influence of wider bilateral and regional challenges on this dispute. It particularly notes the increasingly fraught nature of ties between the two neighbors since the early 2000s, when the optimism of the 1990s was replaced by more 'realism and mixed feelings'. The rise in bilateral frictions over the feature has come in the midst of wider mutual anxieties about the strategic and economic objectives of the other side. China's concerns are mainly security-based in relation to national defense and access to resources. Heightened Republic of Korea (ROK) unease regarding rightful jurisdiction over the feature occurred in a context of growing Chinese influence on the peninsula where South Koreans increasingly felt that a rising China was a threat to Korean sovereignty both north and south and its symbols, touching upon sensitivities concerning national identity and dignity. The chapter discusses the various broader challenges that both states have been attempting to address since the normalization of ties in 1992.

Keywords Bilateral challenges relating to the Socotra Rock dispute • Regional challenges relating to the Socotra Rock dispute • Strategic and economic objectives

Examining the influence of wider bilateral and regional challenges on this dispute particularly reveals the increasingly fraught nature of ties between the two neighbors. This is especially so since the early 2000s,

S. Fox, *China, South Korea, and the Socotra Rock Dispute*,
https://doi.org/10.1007/978-981-13-2077-4_3

when the optimism of the 1990s was replaced, as Synder has put it, by 'more realism and mixed feelings' (Snyder, 2007: 1). The rise in bilateral frictions over the feature has not developed on its own, but has come in the midst of wider mutual anxieties about the strategic and economic objectives of the other side. China's concerns are mainly security-based in relation to national defense and access to resources, and all of this is discussed further in the chapter. Heightened Republic of Korea (ROK) unease regarding rightful jurisdiction over the feature occurred in a context of growing Chinese influence on the peninsula where South Koreans increasingly felt that a rising China was a threat to Korean sovereignty both north and south, as well as its symbols, touching upon sensitivities concerning national identity and dignity. Both states have been attempting to address these various broader challenges since the normalization of ties in 1992. In addition, it presents evidence of a bilateral desire to not allow the issue to damage the wider relationship, and in South Korea's case, to calm domestic anxieties over the feature.

The dispute is also positioned inside the zero-sum game, conflict avoidance-balancing act that exists between the ROK's alliance with the USA and Japan, and its partnership with China. Socotra Rock-related frictions tended to develop in conjunction with maritime tensions elsewhere involving China, such as in the East China Sea vis-à-vis Japan as well as the South China Sea and five other states. Other notable bilateral tensions relate to China's favoritism toward North Korea despite its aggressive activities and historically derived sensitivities regarding China's approach to the peninsula. Examples of this include the 'Revive the Northeast Project' from the early 2000s, and other controversies wherein the Chinese appear to be laying claim to Korean territory, heritage, and artifacts. Anxieties over a possible informal economic domination or even economic colonization, in particular of North Korea, are also a concern, indicating that these events also color how many ordinary and elite South Koreans look upon the Ieodo issue. This all demonstrates how bilateral relations can fluctuate markedly within relatively short time periods. While these relations can improve, and trade and fisheries agreements concluded, Socotra Rock-related tensions still hold the potential to upset broader ties.

The Wider Relationship: 'More Realism and Mixed Feelings'

The rise in bilateral tensions over Socotra Rock emerged in the midst of wider Sino-Korean anxieties about the strategic and economic objectives of each side. This is particularly true in terms of South Korean concerns with the People's Republic of China (PRC)'s growing influence over the Korean Peninsula, both north and south. As Snyder has observed, the 15th anniversary of the normalization of Beijing-Seoul diplomatic ties on 24 August 2007 stood in marked contrast to the 'buoyant lure of mutual economic opportunity' and 'unbridled optimism', which characterized the 10th anniversary in 2002. By 2007, this initial optimism was replaced by, again, Snyder's 'more realism and mixed feelings' of the relationship's future. These mixed emotions continue to be characteristic of relations today.

On the one hand, South Koreans appreciate the critical role that China, as the ROK's largest trading partner, plays and will continue to play in their country's economic development as well as influencing relations with North Korea, and whether that course leads to eventual reunification or not (Roehrig, 2012: 61). Beijing has also carried out an important role in helping Seoul to manage and sometimes reduce North Korea-related threats. China and South Korea also ratified a free trade agreement (FTA) in June 2015 and Beijing promoted the idea of a mutually beneficial trilateral Northeast Asian trade agreement involving China, South Korea, and Japan.[1] All these positive realities provide both strong motivations for closer cooperation with China and strong incentives to avoid potentially destabilizing problems ("Why China Would Compromise", 10/12/2015). At the same time, Seoul finds itself having to balance vital and expanding economic ties with China while managing an equally important military alliance with the USA. As further contended by Chung in 2009, this balancing act between a 'value-based strategic alliance' with the Americans and a 'strategic cooperative partnership' with the Chinese appears increasingly like a zero-sum game (Chung Jae-Ho, 2009: 482).

From the early 1970s until the early 2000s, relations between China and South Korea were generally positive. In the 1980s, openly declared concerns in South Korea over the threat represented by a rising China were rare. Throughout the 1990s there was no such official concern in the

ROK, and this stood in open contrast to Japan, which was well known to have officially listed the PRC as a potential threat. Moreover, the period from 1997 to 2007 was a time when progressives held sway in South Korean domestic politics. This went hand in hand with a perceptible appreciation of the PRC's economic power within the country, thus 'generating positive synergies within Sino-South Korean relations' (Chung Jae-Ho, 2009: 481). This is not to suggest that their ties were bereft of challenging issues, and the 1997 Asian financial crisis and the so-called garlic battle were notable examples. The latter refers to South Korea imposing high tariffs on imports of garlic from the PRC, and the Chinese countered with an import ban on mobile phones and polyethylene from the ROK, thus reflecting the end of the post-1992 'special relationship' honeymoon period and the beginning of a more conventional relationship (Chung Jae-Ho, 2009: 473–474). A gradual change in perceptions inside South Korea toward China became more evident from the early 2000s onward as a number of bilateral disagreements began to sour pre-existing ties.

The Northeast Project and Other Controversies

Included among those bilateral disagreements was the furor surrounding Beijing's 'Revive the Northeast Project' (RNP/NEP) (Dongbei Gongcheng in Chinese) from 2002 to 2007. Launched in February 2002, the central aspect of the Northeast Project controversy was a media uproar over China's stance in regards to the historical Koguryo[2] Dynasty, which lasted from 37 BC to AD 668. Its territory included not only large parts of Manchuria, but also northern and central parts of the Korean Peninsula. The South Korean media widely reported the PRC's position on the issue as representative of a Chinese effort to claim the ancient kingdom. On 24 June 2003, the Guangming Ribao (Guangming Daily), with a largely academic, intellectual readership and a mouthpiece of the Communist Party, reported 'Koguryo was an ancient nation established by a Chinese minority tribe' ("What China's Northeast Project", 30/05/2008), thus undermining widely held opinions that the kingdom was a distinct Korean entity. In terms of timing, this coincided with tensions over the construction of the Ieodo Ocean Research Station in the same month.

There was also bilateral hostility following the South Korean media's disclosure in 2004 that China's state-run research institute, the Chinese Academy of Social Science, had published papers claiming that the ancient Korean kingdom of Koguryo, referred to as Goguryeo in the article, was in fact a vassal state of Zhongguo or what the West calls China's Middle Kingdom. This escalated further when it became known that China was seeking world heritage status from the United Nations Educational, Scientific and Cultural Organization (UNESCO) for the burial sites of Goguryeo kings and had also deleted mention of Goguryeo in an overview of Korean history on their Ministry of Foreign Affairs website. One of South Korea's responses was to create their own Northeast Asia History Foundation to replace the Goguryeo Research Foundation, which was disbanded in August 2006. China's actions appeared to be in contravention of a 2004 oral agreement for easing history-related controversies between China and South Korea (Kwon, 2014). ROK President Roh Moo-hyun expressed regret over the incident while Beijing emphasized that the papers were merely academic documents which did not reflect the PRC's official position ("China Disputes S. Korea's", 14/09/2006). One of the Northeast Project's central objectives was to reinforce and strengthen the economic and ideological ties between the PRC's central authorities in Beijing and the PRC's northeastern corner (Harold, 2012: 295). Professor Song Ki-ho of Seoul National University contended that 'China isn't making the claims just for historical reasons but for political reasons to claim dominion over North Korea in case of a changing political situation in the region' ("What China's Northeast Project", 30/05/2008).

In a region with a large ethnic Korean population, the project sought to weaken any separatist tendencies as well as encourage loyalty to the Chinese state. For South Koreans, the project appeared to be an attempt to undermine their nation's sovereignty as well as the rights of Korean communities abroad. For example, Beijing protested the granting of ROK citizenship to PRC citizens of Korean extraction and went as far as imprisoning and fining returning ethnic Koreans who had acquired ROK citizenship while abroad. The Chinese authorities also insisted on migrants participating in pre-departure education and national allegiance courses (Luova, 2009, 442; Harold, 2012: 295). As noted by Harold, at least one of the policies related to the project 'would appear to infringe directly on Seoul's sovereign right to determine its own citizenship policies and expect that its nationals will not be harassed while abroad solely because of their citizenship'. The Chinese also took measures to discourage expressions of ethnic Korean 'Chosonjuk' identity inside the PRC by promoting the Mandarin language as well as 'pan-ethnic Chinese (zhonghua minzu) nationalism' (Harold, 2012: 295).

The influence of the Northeast Project on South Korean perceptions of China was considerable. In one article, for example, Korea expert Scott Snyder questioned whether 2004 was a possible turning point due to the repercussions of such issues as the NEP (Snyder, 2004: 1). Peter Hays Gries also observed in 2005 how 'Chinese claims that Koguryo is Chinese or was a Chinese vassal state strike at the very heart of what it means to be a Korean today. Koreans perceive [China's claims to Koguyro] as an existential threat' (Hays Gries, 2005: 8).

China's historical claim to Koguryo included appropriating what had been accepted as Korean practices and artifacts as Chinese cultural heritage on UNESCO's World Heritage list. From traditional fourth century Korean wrestling known as *ssiruem* to the folk song '*Arirang*', and from traditional Korean clothing called *hanbok* to a traditional stringed instrument as well as a number of traditional dances and ceremonies, China was seen as having assumed these and more as inherently Chinese. For their part, Beijing insists there are less malicious intentions, and that, for example, these artifacts are to be seen as part of the culture of China's ethnic Koreans ("China lays claim to Arriang", 23/06/2011). In the same period, China, South Korea, and also North Korea submitted competing applications to UNESCO to have locations such as Baekdu/Paektu Mountain,[3] Koguryo artifacts in Jilin and Pyongyang, and traditions such as the Dan'O (Duanwa) Festival recognized as world heritage property (Chung Jae-Ho, 2009: 482). The extent of feeling among South Koreans regarding China's apparent claim to historical Korean territory was reflected in an editorial by an academic from the ROK's Busan National University of Education, Chun Jin-sung in 2007. Writing in the popular *Chosun Ilbo* newspaper, Chun claimed the dispute was not so much about history as it was 'a fear of plunder by strong neighbors' and 'again being cornered' by 'current hegemonism' (Chun, 2007). It is also reported that an opinion poll by the Korean Broadcasting System (KBS), which was conducted immediately after the Koguryo controversy became public, revealed that 58.2 percent of the respondents expressed a dislike for China (Chung Jae-Ho, 2009: 473).[4]

South Koreans are also worried about China's motivations vis-à-vis Beijing's ties with Pyongyang. In relation to both the NEP and North Korea, the Korean journalist Sunny Lee contended in 2011, 'Koreans fear that China's assertion potentially makes much of North Korea its historical territory, and thus could serve as justification for future Chinese claims on North Korea if there is a sudden "upheaval" in the North' (Lee, Sunny,

28/10/2011). Such views inside South Korea were likewise noted in 2011 by John Delury of Yonsei University in Seoul, who observed, 'there is widespread anxiety in South Korea—among government officials, business leaders, and the general public—that China is quietly achieving the economic colonisation of the North, thereby undermining the long-term aspiration for Korean reunification' (Delury, 25/10/2011). It is in this context that observers should appreciate the post-2003 sensitivities over Socotra Rock.

Seoul also protests and refuses to recognize the outcome of PRC-Democratic People's Republic of Korea (DPRK) land and sea border delimitation talks and agreements between Beijing and Pyongyang. Prior to reaching a tacit agreement on the issue, South Korea was also upset about China's cooperation with Pyongyang in the forced repatriation of North Korean refugees inside the PRC and certain imprisonment and torture when they return to the DPRK. Seoul's position is that North Korean refugees should be allowed to travel on to the ROK. This is not to mention PRC resource-related investment deals with the DPRK, as well as the PRC's support for Pyongyang in spite of numerous acts of North Korean aggression against the South (Harold, 2012: 291; 293). According to Harold, the collective effect and danger of these bilateral disagreements and tensions concerns how

> popular and elite anxieties on each side can explode suddenly, driving relations into a tailspin. These disputes have the capacity to shape public opinion and influence leaders' perceptions of themselves and the other. While they often lie dormant in the background, at certain moments they can be thrust forward into the center of public policy debate in either country in ways that may deeply destabilize the bilateral relationship. (Harold, 2012: 305)

Heightened tensions regarding rightful jurisdiction over Socotra Rock took place within a context where South Koreans increasingly felt that China was a threat to Korean sovereignty and its symbols, touching upon emotions and sensitivities concerning national identity and dignity. Unlike national dignity-related disputes with Japan, for example, 'Suyan Rock' tensions have not, as yet, provoked any significant Chinese nationalistic street-level reactions. This is not to say that such ROK-associated challenges cannot or will not produce a strong response from PRC citizens. The recent Terminal High-Altitude Area Defense (THAAD)-inspired economic boycotts of ROK businesses and products (as well as in the area of tourism) provide a notable example.[5]

With the DPRK recommencing nuclear weapons testing in February 2013 after a hiatus of four years, the two neighbors have had to deal with their own bilateral challenges amidst a potentially more serious military threat posed by North Korea. The flip-flop in inter-Korean ties in the 12 months preceding June 2018 is representative of the difficulties attached to anticipating Pyongyang's likely moves in the near future. As explained in more detail in the concluding chapter, North-South relations are presently at their best in over ten years and ties between Beijing and Seoul are thawing after a troublesome spell in 2016 and 2017. In general, however, volatility and turbulence have been the hallmarks of inter-Korean relations historically, so cautious optimism remains the watchword. A notable example of bilateral frictions caused by the DPRK's behavior was the late 2016 announcement by the US and South Korean governments that they would deploy THAAD in order to defend against a possible North Korean missile attack in a future confrontation. Despite US-ROK assertions that THAAD is focused on the North Korean threat, the Chinese fear that the missile defense system and its attendant surveillance systems would place them at a strategic disadvantage and have made no bones about their displeasure with the deployment. At that time, the PRC's ambassador to the ROK, Qiu Guohong, warned that the implementation of THAAD could destroy the bilateral relationship 'in an instant' ("Chinese envoy warns", 24/02/2016). Despite Chinese protestations and a related rise in anti-South Korean sentiment within the PRC, the USA and the ROK installed a THAAD battery on South Korean soil in early 2017.

Since March 2017, the PRC has responded to THAAD-related activities by engaging in economic retaliation and boycotts aimed at punishing South Korea, discussed in a March 2018 article from a regional news source. One of several examples provided is the banning of package tours from China to the ROK. This contributed to an almost 50 percent reduction in the number of Chinese tourists when compared to the previous year. The move cost the South Korean economy ₩5 trillion (US $4.7 billion). While many ROK companies have experienced losses, the highest profile victim of Chinese boycotts has been South Korea's huge Lotte Group conglomerate or chaebol, the country's fifth largest. Often involving anti-THAAD civic groups inside China, the boycotts have seen Lotte suffer major financial losses with 87 of its 99 stores in the PRC temporarily closing, and sales in its remaining Chinese stores falling by over 80 percent. The conglomerate suffered for its role in a land swap deal involving the US and South Korean militaries and a Lotte golf resort on which a THAAD system was to be placed ("S. Korea still smarting", 14/03/2018). As explained in the next section, the Lotte boycott was just one of many cases that have revealed to ordinary South Koreans their country's vulnerability to economic pressure from their giant neighbor. This realization influences and informs the ROK public's sentiments and opinions regarding any perceived PRC assertiveness in relation to Ieodo.[6]

The Role of Economic Ties

Since normalization in 1992, Sino-South Korean economic ties have witnessed immense growth, multiplying by a factor of 18 in terms of trade volume, from US $6.4 billion in 1992 to a staggering US $118 billion in 2006. By 2007, trade ties seemed on course to surpass the US $150 billion mark with forecasts predicting them to go beyond US $200 billion by 2012 (Snyder, 2007: 1). However, by 2011 this figure had in fact grown to US $220.6 billion (Roehrig, 2012: 61). Since 2003, the PRC has been South Korea's largest trading partner and continued to climb as both a source and destination for Chinese and South Korean products (Snyder, 2007: 1). In terms of sources of the PRC's Foreign Direct Investment (FDI), the ROK is its third largest marketplace. As an economy positioned outside the world's top ten, South Korea's potential vulnerability lies in the fact that the PRC, as the world's second largest economy, is the source of nearly one-third of its exports, while the reverse of this, the PRC's reliance on exports to South Korea, the ratio is significantly less (Roehrig, 2012: 61). Despite the earlier mentioned THAAD-related economic losses experienced by the ROK in 2017, its exports to the PRC through July 2017 actually rose to more than US $76.2 billion, which was an 11.5 percent increase from the same period in the previous year (Cho, 20/09/2017).

Figures from 2006 and 2007 are important to consider as 2007 marks the ending of a period of optimism mentioned earlier, and the beginning of 'more realism and mixed feelings'. As of 2007, as many as 43,000 ROK companies enjoyed trading relations with the PRC. In 2006 alone, nearly 10 percent of all South Koreans (3.9 million people) went on tourist trips to China, while as many as 900,000 PRC citizens visited the ROK. The growing imbalance, however, between the quantity (and sometimes poor quality) of cheaper imported PRC goods and exported South Korean products has been an increasing source of frustration and concern, as well as anti-Chinese sentiment. The PRC has also come to dominate the economy of North Korea, strengthening its influence over the entire peninsula and awakening Korean sensitivities regarding their country's history as a vassal kingdom subservient to China (Snyder, 2007: 1).

This sentiment is reflected with regards to Socotra Rock by leading Korean activists such as Yearn-hong Choi when he stated:

> China has its superpower mentality toward Korea, claiming that the ancient kingdom of Goguryeo [37 BCE–668 CE] was part of the Tang Dynasty, and considering North Korea as a colony of China. I don't think its superpower status can make Ieodo part of China. (Choi, 25/06/2010)

Such widely shared views have soured ties and heightened tensions. There has also been a number of high-profile incidents, including the preventable 2007 death of Seoul's number 2 diplomat in Beijing, Whang Joung-il (Snyder, 2007: 5), and violent confrontations between Chinese and South Koreans over fishing incidents in peripheral waters, as discussed subsequently.

Briefly mentioned earlier, anger over the PRC's previous support for Pyongyang and more recent but fluctuating role as advisor or mediator has been and is a constant obstacle in the path of confidence building between Beijing and Seoul. In recent years North Korean nuclear tests have been worrying in addition to a 26 March 2010 torpedo strike on the South Korean naval vessel ROKS *Cheonan*, claiming 46 lives ("'North Korean torpedo' sank South's", 20/05/2010). This was followed about seven months later by a deadly missile attack upon the ROK's Yeonpyeong Island, which killed four people (Kim Deok-hyun, 24/11/2010). All these incidents, amidst China's reluctance to criticize Pyongyang in spite of intense international pressure and condemnation, have raised serious questions among ordinary Koreans about the PRC's goodwill and long-term intentions for the Korean Peninsula. Such fears no doubt inform and influence how South Koreans perceive the rising Chinese dragon's behavior on such issues as Socotra Rock. While policymakers may keep their heads cool, the salience of the 'China Threat' card, should it develop further in the ROK, might tempt power-hungry politicians to exploit a nationalistic issue for their own purposes. As seen in disputes elsewhere in the region, this will only serve to negatively restrict the flexibility with which leaders can approach negotiations.

Fisheries-Related Tensions

Another sticking point between the two neighbors has been issues related to fishing rights in the Yellow Sea and the East China Sea. The absence of an agreed demarcation line between China's and Korea's EEZ has contributed to heightened frictions over the presence of fishing vessels and the legality of their activities in disputed waters. Disagreements over Socotra Rock, overlapping EEZ claims, and illegal fishing are all inter-related. A central cause for concern has been frequent and sometimes fatal physical confrontations between the South Korean Coastguard (also KCG or Korean Coast Guard) and Chinese fishermen casting their nets in disputed waters. This danger, according to one source, has caused ROK decision-makers to view an agreed demarcation of the Yellow Sea as a stabilizing 'catalyst' that might also strengthen the ROK's relationship with China, lead to mutually beneficial development projects, and could have perhaps a positive knock-on effect on South Korea-Japanese delimitation talks that could be to Seoul's advantage (Yoon, 2015: 2).

The implications of the fisheries issue for China should not be underestimated. The PRC's maritime exports industry enjoys total sales of up to US $17.8 billion, about one-third of China's entire agricultural exports (Zhu Jin, 30/05/2012). As explained by Roehrig, the management of fishing stocks and securing a renewable and viable supply of aquatic food sources has also become a 'crucial transnational issue' of global importance (Roehrig, 2012: 71). As a state that has experienced rapid economic growth and urbanization in recent decades, China's per capita consumption of ocean-based food sources has increased from 5 kg in 1970 to 25 kg in 2010 (Zhang, 2012: 1). The results of this demand have included the overfishing of local waters and consequent incursions into neighboring states' EEZs as well as international waters. The depletion of local fishing stocks due to coastal pollution has compounded this shortage (Roehrig, 2012: 71). This has contributed to a greater number of incidents related to the problem of Illegal, Unreported, and Unregulated (IUU) fishing. In early June 2001, Qi Jingfa, the PRC's Vice Minister of Agriculture, acknowledged the extent of the problem in a meeting with Hong Seoung-yong, the ROK's Vice Minister of Maritime and Fisheries. This was followed on 30 June by the establishment of a South Korea-China Joint Fisheries Committee (JFC) ("Sino-South Korea Fishing Agreement", 04/06/2001; Yoon, 2015: 1). It in fact complemented a bilateral accord that had been hammered out three years earlier.

It was in 1998 that Seoul and Beijing had signed the 'Agreement on Fisheries between the Government of the People's Republic of China and the Government of the Republic of Korea', which focused on cooperative fisheries management in the Yellow Sea. The agreement was concluded in August 2000 and actually came into force on 30 June 2001. It designated a Provisional Measures Zone (PMZ) (aka Provisional Waters Zone or PWZ) and two separate Transitional Zones (TZ), one along each state's coastline (Rosenberg 30/06/2005). Both states agreed on three core issues: (a) recognition of coastal EEZ areas and related resource rights; (b) setting up a joint fishing zone where EEZ claims overlapped in the Yellow Sea; and (c) establishment of a shared resources Transitional Zone (TZ) or Interim Co-management Zone for four years.[7] They also set up a Joint Fisheries Commission and agreed to engage in joint surveillance operations to prevent illegal fishing by PRC and ROK fishing vessels (Van Dyke, 2003: 29–30) (Map 3.1).

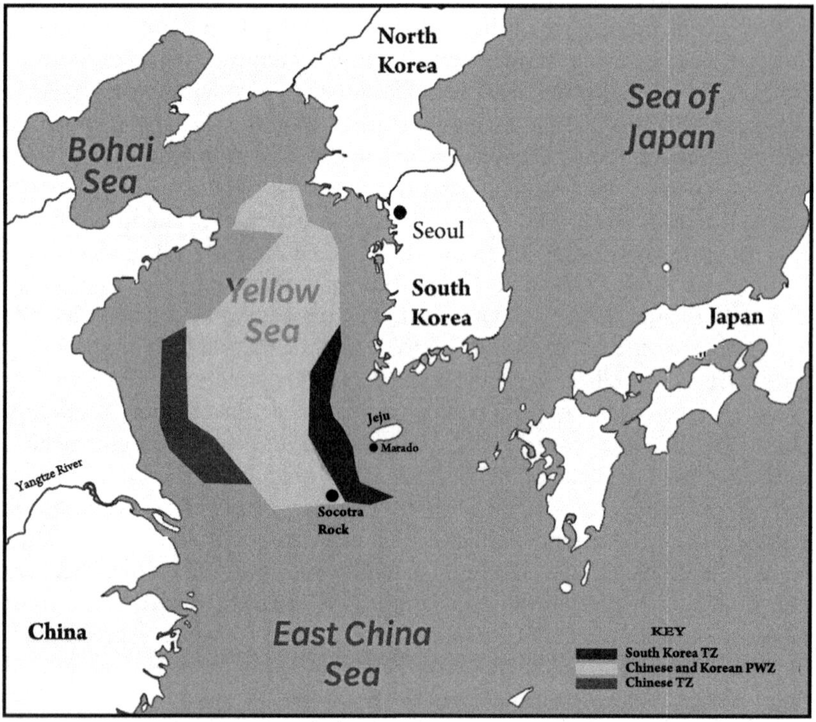

Map 3.1 Socotra Rock and fisheries-related Transitional Zones (TZ) and Provisional Waters Zone (PWZ)

This fisheries agreement was noteworthy because it suggested that the Chinese might concede on the issue of natural prolongation in favor of bilaterally agreed and roughly equidistant demarcation zones related to living resources (Van Dyke, 2003: 30). The agreement was a temporary agreement for four years while both sides hoped that progress might be made in subsequent EEZ delimitation talks. In the absence of a permanent resolution to the demarcation of EEZs in the period 2001–2006, the agreement has since then, however, been renewed every year (Roehrig, 2012: 71). This has not resolved the problem of an increasing number of PRC fishing vessels entering the ROK zones, with occasionally tragic consequences. To provide one example, from 2006 to 2011 as many as 800 Chinese fishermen and more than 2600 Chinese fishing vessels had been reported and processed for fishing illegally inside the ROK's internationally accepted EEZ ("Eradicate illegal fishing", 05/12/2011).

In December 2010, a collision between a Chinese fishing boat and an ROK Coastguard vessel resulted in the deaths of two Chinese fishermen. Beijing criticized Seoul's management of the incident and requested compensation. In October 2011, the ROK Coastguard detained 27 Chinese fishermen from three ships that had been active inside South Korean waters (Roehrig, 2012: 71–72). The Global Times, a widely read mouthpiece for the Communist Party in China, responded angrily to the incident and cautioned Seoul not to 'take [China's] peaceful approach for granted' and warned that if South Koreas do not 'change their ways with China, they will need to prepare for the sounds of cannons' ("Don't Take Peaceful Approach", 25/10/2011).

When an ROK Coast Guard ship detained the crew of a Chinese trawler that had been fishing illegally off the coast of Jeju Island on 19 November 2011, 25 Chinese fishing vessels followed the ship to demand their release (Harold, 2012: 301). And on 12 December, an onboard fight between Chinese fishermen and members of the ROK Coastguard resulted in the death of a South Korean Coastguard officer, the second such fatality since 2008. The fishing boat *Luwenyu 15001* had been fishing illegally in the Yellow Sea, and another official was injured in the incident, which followed an attempt to board the Chinese ship. The ship's captain had stabbed both ROK crew members with a shard of broken glass, and Seoul's response was to detain the crew of nine as well as take possession of their ship. And four months later, on 19 April 2012, a local court in Incheon convicted the crew and sentenced the captain to 30 years in jail and fined him an amount close to US $18,000, or ₩20,000,000. The trial's prosecution team had called for the captain to be executed. The remaining crew members were sentenced to between 18 months to two years in jail

(Roehrig, 2012: 72). The stabbing incident and other similar confrontations inside the ROK's EEZ further heightened negative public opinion in South Korea toward China. Beijing initially expressed regret for the incident and emphasized cooperation with South Korea when investigating the matter. Later, however, the Chinese criticized the court's verdict (Zhang, 20/04/2012). In response to the proceedings, a spokesperson for the PRC's Foreign Ministry Liu Weimin claimed:

> Beijing and Seoul have not achieved an agreement on the definition of related exclusive economic zones, and China does not accept the unilateral resort to the law of exclusive economic zones. ... Beijing will keep a close watch on the case's development and provide necessary assistance to the Chinese citizens involved in the case to ensure their justified and legal rights. (Zhang, 20/04/2012)

What apparently angered China was the use of a disputed EEZ area and South Korea's questionable jurisdiction within that area as the basis for the court's decision rather than ROK domestic law alone (Roehrig, 2012: 72). In May 2012, the ROK's National Assembly passed legislation that would see tougher punishments for illegal fishing activities within South Korean waters, and this included doubling the maximum possible fine to ₩200 million (US$ 176,000) and preventing illegal fishing crews from reclaiming their boats and equipment ("S.Korea toughens penalties", 15/05/2012).

A month later, the two governments agreed to create a joint consultative body which would cooperate in dealing with the IUU problem (Shin Hyon-hee, 08/08/2012). In July 2012, media sources reported that Seoul intended to make an official submission to the United Nations Commission on the Limits of the Continental Shelf (CLCS) claiming an extended area of the East China Sea's continental shelf that went beyond the ROK's EEZ ("S. Korea set to submit formal claim", 22/10/2012). These reports proved true on 26 December 2012 when the ROK government submitted a report to the CLCS, which claimed that their southern continental shelf extends more than 200 nmi all the way to the Okinawa Trough. China had made a similar submission to the CLCS on 14 December 2012 (Park Byong-su, 2013).[8]

A 2013 study used an Automatic Identification System (AIS) to determine, via a receiver on the Ieodo Ocean Research Station (IORS), the nationality of ships, their navigational details, and their activities passing close to Socotra Rock in the period from 21 to 30 November. Vessels sailing under the PRC flag topped the list in terms of frequency, with ROK vessels coming in second. Not unexpectedly, cargo ships and fishing vessels were predominant. The survey concluded that vessels without any apparent flag information were almost certainly Chinese due to the similar navigational routes (with discernible PRC vessels) that they followed (Hong and Yang, 2014: 8). It was 2013 when the ROK Coastguard took hold of more than 180 PRC ships that had been fishing illegally in the Yellow Sea (Keck, 10/10/2014).

In another skirmish between ROK Coast Guard officers and PRC fishermen in early October 2014, one Chinese captain from an illegal vessel was accidentally shot and later died of his injuries while in ROK custody (Tiezzi, 07/11/2015). The officers in question claimed that four other Chinese vessels had attempted to surround and intimidate the ROK Coast Guard ship while the fishermen were accused of using homemade weapons and of trying to strangle one officer (Keck, 10/10/2014). Following the incident, a spokesperson for the PRC's Foreign Ministry, Hong Lei, stated that Beijing was 'deeply shocked by and strongly dissatisfied with such violent law enforcement behavior'. They urged Seoul to 'bring whoever is accountable to justice', and stressed that China 'will continue to follow the incident closely, and urge the ROK side to handle the aftermath in a serious, earnest and proper way' (PRC Foreign Ministry, 10/10/2014).

It was in late November 2015 that the two neighbors held the eighth round of working-level talks on fisheries cooperation. Such working-level talks are held twice a year ("S. Korea, China discuss", 26/11/2015). On 9 December, Beijing and the Chinese media protested an incident in which the South Korean navy fired ten warning shots at a PRC patrol vessel that had crossed in waters disputed by the ROK and DPRK. The South Koreans had apparently mistaken the boat for a North Korean vessel ("China seeks South Korean safety guarantees", 09/12/2015). As a result of this, on 17 December their respective coastguards agreed to establish a maritime hotline and to participate in annual talks in order to prevent any further mishaps and misunderstandings ("S. Korea, China set up", 17/12/2015). EEZ talks resumed on 22 December after a seven-year hiatus, and under the leadership of the PRC's Vice Foreign Minister Liu Zhenmin and his ROK counterpart Cho Tae-yul. Commenting on the meeting, Cho remarked the two sides expected 'difficult and lengthy' discussions because of the legal and technical complexities involved, and stated that a 'fair resolution' was necessary. Liu stated that the meeting was 'historically meaningful'. At the time, both would not comment on whether or not a future meeting had been scheduled ("S. Korea, China hold first talks", 22/12/2015).

The talks came in the context of a positive turn in bilateral relations with President Park Geun-hye cited on 28 December as one of the top ten people of 2015 by Chinese media outlets for her 'balancing' role between China and the USA, as well as her attendance at a Second World War commemorative parade in Beijing in September of that year. Park also saw a rise in her domestic approval rating as a result of these endeavors. This also came on the heels of the implementation of the PRC-ROK FTA on 20 December, which granted South Korea special access to the Chinese market and a much-needed boost for the country's exports (Snyder and Byun, January 2016: 102; 106). Park's subsequent downfall and impeachment based on charges of corruption do not appear to have negatively influenced PRC-ROK relations.

In late June 2016, the ROK Coast Guard dispatched its largest patrol vessel, a 5000-ton cutter, the *Lee Cheong-ho*, named in honor of the officer who was fatally stabbed in December 2011. It was to permanently patrol the waters south of Jeju Island in overlapping EEZ areas as well as to act in a support capacity to the IORS in the event of emergencies and search and rescue missions. At a cost of ₩78.5 billion (US$ 67.9 million), the vessel's primary purpose was and is to watch out for illegal fishing activities, to defend the ROK's territorial waters, and to illustrate Seoul's resolve to defend its national interests at a time when the Chinese and the Japanese had also placed similar-sized vessels in the area ("Korea's Coast Guard stations", 22/06/2016). Professor Lee Jung Nam from Korea University contends that the ROK and the PRC have sought to downplay their Yellow Sea dispute by regularly stating that no territorial dispute exists. Seoul also appreciates that any unnecessary escalation of the dispute could significantly harm the ROK. However, dispatching the patrol vessel *Lee Cheong-ho* was arguably a reflection of South Korean frustration at official and public levels over high-profile incidents involving illegal fishing vessels from the PRC (Zhen, 23/06/2016). In spite of this, China and South Korea reached a memorandum of understanding in December 2015 and held the first regular meeting between their two countries' coastguard services in June 2016. They also agreed to hold the tenth ROK-PRC meeting on fisheries cooperation sometime in the latter half of 2016 (ROK Foreign Ministry, 05/07/2016).

In spite of such meetings, hotlines, and fisheries agreements, the waters around and in proximity to Socotra Rock are still contentious. In September 2016 three Chinese fishermen died in a boat fire after personnel on a pursuing KCG vessel threw flash grenades onto their ship. In October, illegal fishermen rammed their ships into a coastguard ship and sank it. As recently as December 2017, the ROK coast guard fired 249 warning shots at Chinese ships allegedly engaged in illegal fishing (Shin Hyon-hee, 20/12/2017). All of these incidents served to remind observers of the potential of such standoffs and clashes between the vessels of the two neighbors to end tragically with negative consequences for the development of solid bilateral ties. They also serve to illustrate the importance of both sides reaching an accommodation or resolution vis-à-vis Socotra Rock.[9] Notable incidents directly related to the submerged rock as well as attempts to reach agreements are discussed in the next chapter.

Notes

1. This took place in Tokyo, May 2018; see Mainichi Shimbun, 10/05/2018, 'Japan, China agree on economic cooperation but differ over objectives', https://mainichi.jp/english/articles/20180510/p2a/00m/0na/003000c.
2. *Gaogouli* in Chinese.
3. Also *Changbaishan* in Chinese.
4. See http://www.kas.de/wf/doc/kas_19560-1522-2-30.pdf?110608104012; 167.
5. For further insights and perspectives on the ebb and flow of popular sentiment and the influence of social media toward South Korea inside China, see any of the following: Frances Kitt, (11/05/2017), 'In China, changing online attitudes towards Korea', *The Interpreter*, Lowy Institute: https://www.lowyinstitute.org/the-interpreter/china-changing-online-attitudes-towards-korea; Sunny Lee, (24/08/2008), 'Anti-Korean Sentiment in China Overshadows Lee-Hu Summit Today', *Korea Times*: http://www.koreatimes.co.kr/www/news/sports/2009/04/253_29884.html; Sunny Lee, (09/03/2008), 'Anti-Korean Sentiment in China Evolutionary', *Korea Times*: https://web.archive.org/web/20120918115733/http://www.koreatimes.co.kr/www/news/include/print.asp?newsIdx=30480; Moon Chung-in and Li Chun-fu (30/11/2010), 'Reactive Nationalism and South Korea's Foreign Policy on China and Japan: A Comparative Analysis', *Pacific Focus Inha Journal of International Studies* 25, no. 3: 331–355: https://onlinelibrary.wiley.com/doi/pdf/10.1111/j.1976-5118.2010.01048.x; Scott Snyder, (October 2008), 'Post-Olympic Hangover: New Backdrop for Relations', *Comparative*

Connections 10, Issue 3: http://cc.csis.org/wp-content/uploads/2017/05/0803qchina_korea.pdf.

6. See, for example Hong Soon-do, 'Lotte Faces Boycott in China due to THAAD Conflict', 25 January 2018: https://www.huffingtonpost.com/asiatoday/lotte-faces-boycott-in-ch_b_14382948.html; Cynthia Kim and Hyunjoo Jin, 'Chinese Envoy Warns THAAD Deployment Would "Destroy" Ties', 24 February 2016: https://www.reuters.com/article/us-lotte-china-analysis/with-china-dream-shattered-over-missile-land-deal-lotte-faces-costly-overhaul-idUSKBN1CT35Y; Ankit Panda, 'What Is THAAD, What Does It Do, and Why Is China Mad About It?' 25 February 2016: https://thediplomat.com/2016/02/what-is-thaad-what-does-it-do-and-why-is-china-mad-about-it/.
7. The shared resources zone was to be approximately 17.5 nmi on each side of the Provisional Waters Zone for four years, after which the zones would be split down the middle, with each half falling under the exclusive state control of the nearest country.
8. See http://www.un.org/depts/los/clcs_new/submissions_files/submission_kor_65_2012.htm.
9. Seehttps://thediplomat.com/2016/10/when-chinese-fishermen-become-pirates-in-the-yellow-sea/; https://www.nytimes.com/2016/10/01/world/asia/south-korea-china-fishermen-deaths.html.

Bibliography

China disputes S. Korea's ownership of Ieo Island (14/09/2006), *Hankyoreh.* http://english.hani.co.kr/arti/english_edition/e_international/157139.html

China Lays Claim to 'Arirang' (23/06/2011), *Chosun Ilbo.* http://english.chosun.com/site/data/html_dir/2011/06/23/2011062301297.html

China seeks South Korean safety guarantees after warning shots fired at ship (09/12/2015), *Reuters.* http://www.reuters.com/article/us-china-south-korea-idUSKBN0TS0TA20151209

Chinese Envoy Warns THAAD Deployment Would 'Destroy' Ties (24/02/2016), *Chosun Ilbo.* http://english.chosun.com/site/data/html_dir/2016/02/24/2016022401747.html

Cho, Kye-wan. "South Korea sees biggest worldwide growth in exports in first half of 2017." 20/09/2017. http://english.hani.co.kr/arti/english_edition/e_business/811841.html

Choi, Yearn-hong. 'Ieodo.' *Korea Times*, 25/06/2010. http://www.koreatimes.co.kr/www/news/opinon/2011/04/137_68269.html

Chun, Jin-sung. "Our Dispute with China Isn't About Ancient History." *Chosun Ilbo*, 27/02/2007. http://english.chosun.com/site/data/html_dir/2007/02/27/2007022761035.html

Chung, Jae Ho. "China's "Soft" Clash With South Korea: The History War And Beyond," *Asian Survey* 49, no. 3 (May/June 2009): 468–483.

Delury, John. "North Korea Rents Out Its Resources to Stave Off Reform." *New York Times*, 25/10/2011. http://www.nytimes.com/2011/10/26/world/asia/north-korea-rents-out-its-resources-to-stave-off-reform.html

Don't Take Peaceful Approach for Granted (25/10/2011), *Global Times*. http://www.globaltimes.cn/content/680694.shtml

Eradicate illegal fishing by Chinese boats in Korean EEZ (05/12/2011), *Yonhap News Agency*. http://english.yonhapnews.co.kr/yhedit/2011/12/05/88/5100000000AEN20111205007600315F.html

Gries, Peter Hays. "The Koguryo Controversy, National Identity, and Sino-Korean Relations Today," *East Asia* 22, Winter 2005, Issue 4, (Winter 2005): 3–17. https://doi.org/10.1007/s12140-005-0001-y

Harold, Scott W. "Ieodo as Metaphor? The Growing Importance of Sovereignty Disputes in South Korea–China Relations and the Role of the United States," *Asian Perspective* 36, no. 2 (April–June 2012): 287–307.

Hong, Danbee and Chan-Su Yang. "Classification of Passing Vessels Around the Ieodo Ocean Research Station Using Automatic Identification System," *Journal of the Korean Society for Marine Environment and Energy* 17, no. 4 (November 2014): 1–9. https://doi.org/10.7846/JKOSMEE.12014.17.4.1

Keck, Zachary. "Chinese Fisherman Killed By South Korea's Coast Guard." *The Diplomat*, 10/10/2014. https://thediplomat.com/2014/10/chinese-fisherman-killed-by-south-koreas-coast-guard/

Kim, Deok-hyun. "S. Korea to toughen rules of engagement against N. Korean attack." *Yonhap News*, 24/11/2010. http://english.yonhapnews.co.kr/national/2010/11/24/86/0301000000AEN20101124012200315F.html

Korea's Coast Guard stations 5,000-ton patrol ship south of Jeju (22/06/2016), *Korea Herald*. http://www.koreaherald.com/view.php?ud=20160622000911

Kwon, Yong. "Korea and China's Clashing Histories." *The Diplomat*, 11/07/2014. https://thediplomat.com/2014/07/korea-and-chinas-clashing-histories/

Lee, Sunny. "Should Korea, China Tackle Sensitive Goguryeo Issue?" *Korea Times*, 28/10/2011. http://www.koreatimes.co.kr/www/news/nation/2014/04/116_97528.html

Luova, Outi. "Transnational Linkages and Development Initiatives in Ethnic Korean Yanbian, Northeast China: "Sweet and Sour" Capital Transfers." *Pacific Affairs* 82, no. 3 (Fall, 2009): 427–446.

'North Korean torpedo' sank South's Navy Ship – Report (20/05/2010), *BBC News*. http://www.bbc.com/news/10129703

Park, Byong-su. "South Korea claims larger continental shelf." *Hankyoreh*, 09/01/2013. http://english.hani.co.kr/arti/english_edition/e_international/568898.html

PRC Foreign Ministry. Press Conference, 10/10/2014. http://www.fmprc.gov.cn/ce/cegh/eng/fyrth/t1199361.htm

Roehrig, Terence. "Republic of Korea Navy and China's Rise: Balancing Competing Priorities." In *CNA Maritime Asia Project Workshop Two: Naval Developments in Asia*, edited by Michael A. McDevitt and Catherine K. Lea, 61–78. Alexandria, Va.: Center for Naval Analyses, 2012.

Rosenberg, David. "China, neighbors progress in fishery agreements."Asia Times Online, 19/08/2005. http://www.atimes.com/atimes/China/GH19Ad02.html

ROK Ministry of Foreign Affairs. Press Briefing, 05/07/2016.

S. Korea, China discuss illegal fishing problem (26/11/2015), *Korea Times.* http://www.koreatimes.co.kr/www/news/nation/2016/05/113_191890.html

S. Korea, China hold first talks on EEZs in 7 years (22/12/2015), *Yonhap News Agency.* http://english.yonhapnews.co.kr/national/2015/12/22/0301000000AEN20151222002053315.html

S. Korea, China set up coast guards' hotline (17/12/2015), *Yonhap News Agency.* http://english.yonhapnews.co.kr/news/2015/12/17/0200000000AEN20151217007300315.html

S. Korea set to submit formal claim on East China Sea shelf to U.N (22/10/2012), *Yonhap News Agency.* http://english.yonhapnews.co.kr/national/2012/10/22/7/0301000000AEN20121022003900315F.html

S. Korea still smarting from China's THAAD retribution (14/03/2018), *Yonhap News Agency.* http://english.yonhapnews.co.kr/news/2018/03/14/0200000000AEN20180314002700320.html

S. Korea toughens penalties for EEZ violation (15/05/2012), *Yonhap News Agency.* http://english.yonhapnews.co.kr/national/2012/05/15/34/0302000000AEN20120515001800320F.html

Shin, Hyon-hee. "Spats mar 20 years of China ties." *Korea Herald*, 08/08/2012. http://www.koreaherald.com/view.php?ud=20120808001121

Shin, Hyon-hee. "South Korea fires 249 warning shots at Chinese ships suspected of carrying out illegal fishing in its waters." *The Independent*, 20/12/2017. https://www.independent.co.uk/news/world/asia/south-korea-chinese-finish-boats-warning-shots-illegal-fishing-waters-a8119871.html

Sino-South Korea Fishing Agreement to Take Effect (04/06/2001), *People's Daily.* http://www.china.org.cn/english/10470.htm

Snyder, Scott. "A Turning Point for China–Korea Relations", *Comparative Connections* 6, no. 3 (July–Sept 2004). http://cc.csis.org/2004/10/turning-point-china-korea-relations/

Snyder, Scott. "China-Korea Relations: Teenage Angst: 15th Anniversary of Diplomatic Relations." *Comparative Connections* (October 2007). http://cc.csis.org/2007/10/teenage-angst-15th-anniversary-diplomatic-relations/

Snyder, Scott and See-won Byun. "China-Korea Relations: A Complex China-ROK Partnership." Comparative Connections 17, no. 3 (January 2016): 97–108.

Tiezzi, Shannon. "Is China Ready to Solve One of Its Maritime Disputes?" *The Diplomat*, 07/11/2015. http://thediplomat.com/2015/11/is-china-ready-to-solve-one-of-its-maritime-disputes/

Van Dyke, Jon M. "The Republic of Korea's Maritime Boundaries," Honolulu, Hawaii: *William S. Richardson School of Law*, University of Hawaii at Manoa, 2003. http://webcache.googleusercontent.com/search?q=cache:F8E1lcIosdsJ:www.hawaii.edu/elp/publications/faculty/TheRepublicofKorea.doc+&cd=1&hl=ja&ct=clnk&gl=jp

What China's Northeast Project Is All About (30/05/2008), *Chosun Ilbo*. http://english.chosun.com/site/data/html_dir/2008/05/30/2008053061001.html

Why China Would Compromise in the Yellow Sea (10/12/2015), *Stratfor Worldview*. https://www.stratfor.com/analysis/why-china-would-compromise-yellow-sea?utm_source=Twitter&utm_medium=Official&utm_campaign=Link

Yoon, Sukjoon. "Korea-China Maritime Boundary Talks: Implications for South China Sea." *RSIS Commentary* No. 89, 13 April 2015. https://www.rsis.edu.sg/wp-content/uploads/2015/04/CO15089.pdf

Zhang, Hongzhou. "China's Growing Fishing Industry and Regional Maritime Security," *S. Rajaratnam School of International Studies Commentaries* (2 June 2012). https://www.rsis.edu.sg/rsis-publication/idss/1753-chinas-growing-fishing-indu/#.WluGsq5l_Z4

Zhang, Yunbi. "ROK's verdict on captain rejected." *China Daily*, 20/04/2012. http://wo.chinadaily.com.cn/view.php?mid=68604&cid=88&isid=809

Zhen, Liu. "South Korea deploys new coastguard ship to watch waters around disputed Ieodo islet." *South China Morning Post*, 23/06/2016. http://www.scmp.com/news/china/diplomacy-defence/article/1979992/south-korea-deploys-new-coastguard-ship-watch-waters

Zhu, Jin. "Group Formed To Aid Fisheries." *China Daily*, 30/05/2012. http://usa.chinadaily.com.cn/china/2012-05/30/content_15418381.htm

CHAPTER 4

Recent Controversies and Agreements

Abstract Here, pertinent controversies and agreements directly related to Socotra Rock since the late 1980s are discussed in detail. The chapter demonstrates that while China has repeatedly protested South Korean activities in the area, it was not until the mid-1990s, when the two neighbors ratified the United Nations Convention on the Law of the Sea (UNCLOS) and set their Exclusive Economic Zone (EEZ) and continental shelf claims in stone, that the dispute slowly developed into the bilateral challenge of today. Alongside mutual reassurances, China issued protests against any unilateral activities in the overlapping area, stating they 'can't take any legal effect'. Its more assertive and physical responses to Seoul's activities since 2003 are also described, consisting of contradictory declarations at various People's Republic of China (PRC) governmental levels, and a shift away from purely diplomatic protests. In addition to displays of jurisdictional authority, the Chinese adopted stronger language in a context where they viewed the relative strength of their jurisdictional claims as weakening.

Keywords Socotra Rock agreements • Socotra Rock controversies • United Nations Convention on the Law of the Sea (UNCLOS)

The controversies and agreements directly related to Socotra Rock since the late 1980s are certainly worth some detailed consideration. While China repeatedly protested South Korean activities in the area, it was not

S. Fox, *China, South Korea, and the Socotra Rock Dispute*,
https://doi.org/10.1007/978-981-13-2077-4_4

until the mid-1990s, when the two neighbors ratified the United Nations Convention on the Law of the Sea (UNCLOS) and set their Exclusive Economic Zone (EEZ) and continental shelf claims in stone, that the dispute slowly developed into the bilateral challenge of today. Alongside mutual reassurances, China issued protests against any unilateral activities in the overlapping area, stating they 'can't take any legal effect'. Its more assertive and physical responses to Seoul's activities since 2003 are also notable, consisting of contradictory declarations at various People's Republic of China (PRC) governmental levels, and a shift away from purely diplomatic protests.

In addition to displays of jurisdictional authority, the Chinese adopted stronger language in a context where they viewed the relative strength of their jurisdictional claims as weakening. The subsequent years, particularly from 2006 onward, thus represented a new chapter in Socotra Rock-related ties, which also reflected the new strategic and security environment in which the two neighbors found themselves. The setting up of South Korean non-governmental organizations (NGOs) aimed at better defending their country's Socotra Rock claims as well as public demonstrations of resolve by the Republic of Korea (ROK)'s naval and air forces also merit some attention. Just how the controversy tapped into a central security worry for South Korea and indeed any state which has a maritime dispute with China was an important shift, relating to the uninterrupted freedom of navigation and peaceful activity within a state's EEZ as the number of Chinese vessels in the said area increased. The higher number of sometimes fatal clashes between Chinese fishing vessels and the ROK coastguard in the Yellow Sea proved to be a significant factor. Seoul's fears in this regard seemed to be confirmed in 2011 when Chinese authorities, emphasizing their EEZ claim, demanded that the South Koreans receive approval from the PRC before commencing the salvage operation for a sunken ship.

Initial Clashes

This began in 1987, which marks the opening phase of a series of artificial developments on and around Socotra Rock. It commenced when the Korean Maritime and Port Administration attached a lighted buoy to the rock so as to warn passing ships of the feature's presence. Considering that it was more than 35 years since the Korean Alpine Club had placed a copper plate on the feature to claim it for Korea, this lighted buoy was an extraordinary event and its placement was publicly announced in press releases by the South Korean government (Korea Hydrographic and Oceanographic Agency, 2010). This seemingly innocuous act did not elicit any strong response from China at the time. Indeed, while the PRC had repeatedly protested Korean activities in the area, it was not until the mid-1990s that the Socotra Rock dispute first slowly developed into the bilateral challenge which both states still face today. In a period when UN member states were ratifying UNCLOS and legally defining EEZs and continental shelf rights, South Korea's Ministry of Land, Transport, and Maritime Affairs started to make plans for substantial construction activities on the submerged rock in the face of Beijing's stated protests (Surhone et al., 2010: 1; Choi, 25/06/2010; "China disputes S. Korea's ownership", 14/09/2006). The PRC[1] and the ROK[2] ratified UNCLOS in June 1996 and January 1996, respectively (Song Yann-huei, 2012: 29).[3] The current Ieodo Ocean Research Station, completed in 2003 and including a helicopter landing pad and state-of-the-art monitoring and scientific facilities, now towers above the sea, the product of planning carried out between 1995 and 2001, for the ostensible purpose of gathering data on ocean currents, weather patterns, and fisheries (Surhone et al., 2010: 1; Choi, 25/06/2010; "China disputes S. Korea's ownership", 14/09/2006).

During that period, Seoul also declared claims to other areas of the northern East China Sea. For example, when Japan and the PRC concluded their symbolic Fisheries Agreement in 2000, though begun in 1998, South Korea reminded the two states of the continuing problem of overlapping EEZs in the northern East China Sea. Seoul proposed that in the future they should hold trilateral negotiations in order to address their delimitation disagreements. In 2000, some progress on Socotra Rock issue was made when Seoul and Beijing publicly declared their consensus that the feature was, in legal terms, a submerged rock and thus not an island entitled to its own territorial waters. Even though this declaration stated the obvious, it helped to cool tensions regarding the nature of the dispute. Importantly, both countries were outlining their position that the disagreement was over EEZs and not related to the more inflammatory issue of sovereignty (Drifte, 18/03/2009). Such declarations have become regular in recent years. Alongside mutual reassurances, however, the Chinese government issued protests against any unilateral activities in the overlapping area, including the research station's construction, doing so at least twice between 2000 and 2002 (PRC Foreign Ministry, 14/09/2006).

The Korean Ocean Research and Development Institute (KORDI)[4] formally named the feature Ieodo in February 2000, and the National Geographic Information Institute[5] finally approved the feature's official name and anglicized it in January 2001 (Kang Byeong-Cheol, 2012: 215; Chin, 03/02/2014). The submerged rock was then officially designated by the Korea Institute of Geology as Ieodo in January 2001 (Surhone et al., 2010: 2). Later that same year, Seoul contributed ₩21.2 billion (US $25.7 million) to the building of the Ieodo Ocean Research Station (Wang Manna, 26/08/2007). According to Kang, there were two central reasons for Seoul's support for this relatively expensive project, one concerning practical issues and the other being more political. Regarding the former, the IORS would strengthen South Korea's capabilities in terms of weather forecasting and maritime safety in advance of storms and typhoons, as well as in regards to maritime resource protection and conservation. In addition, the Ieodo Ocean Research Station (IORS) helps to ensure freedom of movement and safe passage for the thousands of ships that pass through vital Sea Lines of Communication (SLOCs) in the Yellow Sea and the East China Sea each year. The second reason was to place South Korea in a stronger role in terms of addressing any future uncertainties in the waters around the submerged feature (Kang Byeong-Cheol, 2012: 215–216). While South Korea might deny it, others claim a strong motivation for the development would have been strengthening their state's claim to the feature in accordance with UNCLOS guidelines for EEZ and continental shelf rights. When these developments first began, Chinese responses to the upsurge in activities in the area were largely confined to diplomatic protests. This was not to last, however, and Chinese responses increased. As discussed in the next section, the subsequent years, particularly from 2006 onward, would represent a new chapter in Socotra Rock-related ties, which arguably reflected the new strategic and security environment in which the two neighbors now found themselves.

More Assertive Responses by China

After 2002, the Chinese maintained a closer watch on South Korea's actions in relation to Socotra Rock, and stepped up their diplomatic protests and responses. This was probably because the relative strength of its claim over the rock issue was viewed as diminishing ever since Seoul intensified its developments on and around the feature. In 2006, for example, PRC planes carried out an increased number of surveillance over-flights above the South Korean research station. According to a report displayed on the home page of China's State Oceanic Administration (SOA), PRC aircraft commissioned by the SOA carried out aerial surveillance over IORS on five occasions in 2006 alone. This was the first time ever that the Chinese had carried out such operations. The activities also led to media speculation in South Korea that the Chinese were preparing to formally lay claim to the feature and that these actions represented the opening salvo in a diplomatic offensive aimed at strengthening the PRC's claim ("China Chafes at Korean Observatory", 14/09/2006; "China disputes S. Korea's ownership", 14/09/2006). September 2006 also saw Beijing referring to South Korean activities in the area as 'illegal' and being more vocal in its opposition to any 'unilateral' actions. On 14 September 2006, for example, the PRC's Foreign Ministry spokesperson, Qin Gang, informed the media that China and Korea's EEZs overlapped at Socotra Rock and that the Chinese government objected to any 'unilateral' and 'illegal' activities carried out by South Korea in the area. Qin, however, also emphasized how both states agreed that no 'territorial' dispute ever existed over the feature. He nonetheless declared that Chinese and South Korean officials had met on two occasions prior to the station's completion in 2003 without reaching an agreement on a sea border, and as such 'we have never determined its ownership with South Korea' ("China Chafes at Korean Observatory", 14/09/2006; "China disputes S. Korea's ownership", 14/09/2006). The Chinese spokesperson further elaborated on the PRC's position:

> In handling its relations with other countries, China abides by universally-recognized norms of international laws and advocates consultations and dialogues. Suyan islet is located in the northern part of East China Sea under the sea level, over which China and the ROK have no territorial disputes. China and the ROK have conducted several consultations over the demarcation of each others' exclusive economic zones. Suyan islet is located in an area over which both countries have overlapping EEZ claims. In 2000 and 2002, China made representations twice to the ROK for its construction of the maritime observation station on Suyan islet and opposed its unilateral actions in the area over which both countries have overlapping exclusive economic zones claims. The ROK said Suyan islet wouldn't affect the demarcation of the exclusive economic zones. China always holds a clear and consistent position on Suyan islet. ROK's unilateral actions can't take any legal effect. (PRC Foreign Ministry, 14/09/2006)

Soon afterward, a South Korean government representative also explained the bilateral problem by saying, 'Basically, it is not a territorial dispute, but a problem caused by the absence of a firm exclusive economic zone between the two countries'. He added, 'Clearly, Ieo Island is part of South Korea's sovereign rights. Thus it is our lawful right to build and operate a maritime scientific base upon it' ("China disputes S. Korea's ownership", 14/09/2006). An official at South Korea's embassy in Beijing also responded to China's position by declaring that Ieodo was within the ROK's EEZ by virtue of the fact that its nearest territory is South Korean and because it sits on the Korean continental shelf ("China Chafes at Korean Observatory", 14/09/2006).

In the 26 November 2006 edition of *Asia Week* or *Yazhou Zhoukan* (亞洲周刊), a news magazine based in Hong Kong, a report was published about a Chinese NGO, the Suyan Rock Protection Association. It was headed by a Chinese Social Science Academy graduate student, identified in the *Korea Times* as Wang Chien-Hsing (Zienshing). The association had been established for the purposes of conducting activities aimed at emphasizing China's rights to Socotra Rock. In the article, Wang asserted that the feature was Chinese and called upon Chinese people to destroy the IORS. He also claimed that China had reportedly prepared a bronze plaque with the words 'Territory of China' written on it and intended to place it on the feature. Wang also stated that he had sent a letter to the ROK's embassy in Beijing demanding that Seoul dismantle and remove the IORS (Kang Byeong-Cheol, 2012: 219). Interestingly, this episode is one of the few examples of Chinese nationalist reaction to Socotra Rock available in English.

On 4 August 2007, less than three weeks before the 15th anniversary of the normalization of bilateral ties, the PRC's SOA, as an administrative agency under the control of the PRC's Ministry of Land Resources, created confusion and concern when it affirmed China's claim to 'Suyan Rock' (Snyder, 2007: 8). The SOA's purpose is to supervise coastal management and ocean environment projects as well as to draft the state's maritime policies and laws. The body also has certain policing powers, which allow it to enforce laws and regulations (State Oceanic Administration, 2014). The assertion was outlined in an article in an SOA journal publication, declaring that Seoul's activities on the feature were encroaching upon the PRC's sovereignty and that 'Suyan Rock is [an] inseparable [part] of China'. It was also argued that the primary motives behind the research station on Socotra Rock were 'political and military'

(Do Je-hae, 28/09/2014). The SOA's comments caused confusion because they did not indicate whether the claim to the feature was sanctioned by the Ministry of Land Resources or the SOA itself, and whether or not it had the approval of the central government. The uncertainty concerning whether the SOA had the power to promulgate regulations on its own only added to South Korean concerns about Beijing's actual stance in this dispute. Nonetheless, as Van Dyke contends, even if the article was published without the approval of the central government, it left no doubts about where the SOA stood (Van Dyke, 2011: 14). Following the SOA's claims to the feature, the South Korean Congress of Cheju Special Self-Governing Province quickly responded by officially reaffirming Socotra Rock by referring to its Korean name, Ieodo, on 7 August 2007. The Congress also designated 18 January as Ieodo Day. An article in the *Epoch Times* reported in late August that, as a result, hundreds of enraged nationalistic PRC citizens in areas such as Beijing and Jiangsu, for example, were trying to apply to the Ministry of Civil Affairs for the purpose of registering as members of a new organization, and to form a group before the end of the month known as the 'Chinese Association to Defend Suyan Rock'. According to the same article, if their attempts at registration were successful, the group intended to raise money to purchase a boat to then sail to the rock, thus emphasizing the PRC's sovereignty over it. It noted as well, however, that with the October 2007 Seventeenth National Congress of the Communist Party of China approaching, the political atmosphere was sensitive, and successful registration was not assured (Wang Manna, 26/08/2007). By 2008, although the group had not been able to register, the two governments had held as many as ten rounds of negotiations aimed at agreeing on definite EEZs, but with no compromise in sight (Jung, 08/08/2008).

At the same time, trouble flared up again when Seoul discovered that the website of a state agency in the PRC had a section which described Socotra Rock as 'Suyan Rock' in Chinese and as part of China's territory. It also stated that the submerged rock's location was within the PRC's EEZ. This prompted a senior official at the South Korean Ministry of Foreign Affairs and Trade to state that 'the internet site referring to Ieodo as Chinese territory is against the agreement. So, we will take necessary measures to rectify the territorial claim, including demanding the Chinese Foreign Ministry correct the record.' As a consequence, he declared that Seoul would ask Beijing to rectify the description. The official went on to dismiss the Chinese website's claim and asserted 'Ieodo is located 81 nautical miles southwest of our island of Marado, and 147 nautical miles northeast of China. There is no doubt that Ieodo is in our EEZ' (Jung, 08/08/2008).

During this general time period, the heightened tensions with China over Socotra Rock after 2006 spurred a number of Korean scholars and activists into establishing the Seoul-based Society for Ieodo Research (SIR). This had originated in 2007 at Jeju National University under the direction of leading Ieodo activist and President of SIR, Koh Choong-suk. It was established for the purposes of promoting research in the fields of law, geology, oceanography, the arts, and mythology in ways that would support South Korea's claims to Ieodo (Choi, 25/06/2010). This along with the Chinese website saga of 2008 only intensified Korean efforts to draw attention to the dispute among ordinary citizens. Koh, for example, has written numerous articles on the issue which have appeared in South Korean newspapers. These responses should also be seen in the context of tensions with Japan over the Liancourt Rocks. In one effort to explain, Koh was quoted as having justified the setting up of SIR by saying 'Back in 2007, the Japanese government stepped up its claim over the Dokdo islets [Liancourt Rocks]. I was serving as president of Jeju National University back then. I thought I needed to do something to protect our territory' (Kang Hyun-kyung, 12/10/2010). At the defense level, Korean eagerness to assertively defend its EEZ was also reflected in small ways. For example, there was a 2007 decision to officially change the Japanese language name of the 'Hyuga shou' or Hyuga Reef, named after a Japanese battleship sunk in 1927, to the Korean title, Gageocho (Gageo Reef). The completely submerged feature, referred to as Rixiang Jiao (Rixiang Reef in Chinese, a variant of the original Japanese) sits 7.8 meters below the water and within an overlapping EEZ area with China in the Yellow Sea. To Beijing's chagrin, Seoul also completed construction of an Ieodo type research station on the feature in 2009 (Han, 13/10/2009).

Salvage Operation Controversy

Developments surrounding the South Korean salvaging of a sunken ship near Socotra Rock in June and July 2011 further escalated tensions. The Chinese responses to Korean salvage efforts reflected increased concerns from the central government about a peaceful and consistent approach to this disagreement in the absence of an agreed EEZ boundary. The affair revolved around a salvage operation relating to a 50,905-ton Jeju coal carrying bulk carrier, *Oriental Hope*, which had sunk in April 2011 in an area 0.8 km southwest of Socotra Rock.

According to the Korean Ministry of Foreign Affairs and Trade (MOFAT),[6] a number of tugboats and barges were in the area as part of a joint operation involving the sunken ship, which included a Korean manufacturer and a Dutch salvage company. A central security worry for not only South Korea, but virtually any state which has a maritime dispute with the PRC, is the uninterrupted freedom of navigation and peaceful activity within one's perceived EEZ. Seoul's fears in this regard seemed to be confirmed when Chinese authorities, emphasizing their EEZ claim, demanded that South Korea receive approval from the PRC before commencing the salvage operation for the sunken ship ("China sent gov't vessel", 27/07/2011).

An ROK newspaper reported the incident as one where the PRC forced a Korean salvage vessel to suspend its operations until further notice. On three occasions (13 June, 2 July, and 5 July), the Chinese ordered patrol ships into the area and radioed a South Korean ship involved in the salvage operation. The PRC vessel then warned the ship's crew that they were engaged in unauthorized activities within China's EEZ waters and would have to request a permit. In response, the ROK ship contacted the Seogwipo City Maritime Police in southern Jeju island to inform them of what was happening. Shortly afterward, the arrival of a 3000-ton Korean patrol vessel moderated tensions. On 5 July, the relevant authorities on Jeju informed the Chinese personnel that the salvage operation had nothing to do with the PRC, and that the Korean vessel had already received approval from the ROK government. The salvage operation continued uninterrupted. The Seogwipo City Maritime Police also maintained a regular watch at the scene after early July in case of any further trouble ("China sent gov't vessel", 27/07/2011; "Military holds course", 08/03/2012).

In response to the incidents, the Chinese patrol ships withdrew from the area after they learned that South Korean Coast Guard vessels were en route ("China demands S. Korea stop", 27/07/2011). The ROK's Foreign Ministry also received a report on the entire incident. They were, however, unwilling to discuss the matter further with the media or to disclose any more details, most likely out of concern that the affair could upset more important ties between the two countries ("China sent gov't vessel", 27/07/2011). For example, following the incident, a South

Korean Foreign Ministry official publicly declared that 'There was no particular dispute with China with regard to Ieodo' and that 'Hoisting work is continuing as the two sides agreed to deal with the issue without disputes' ("China demands S. Korea stop", 27/07/2011; Shin Hae-in, 27/07/2011).

What some might term as China's 'interference' in a legitimate Korean operation within the ROK's EEZ ended up tapping into growing anxieties concerning an apparent intensification of PRC assertions vis-à-vis Ieodo since 2006. Even before the June and July 2011 salvage incident became public knowledge, a nationalistic albeit 'tongue in cheek' South Korean website, *Dokdo Times*, warned visitors of the dangers posed by the Chinese dragon over issues such as Ieodo. In this regard, the author asserted 'Japan was never likely to fight over Dokdo whereas China will actually need to fight minor wars in the next few years in order to create the sense of nationalism necessary to hold the fractious failed state together'. The site content went on to argue that James Cameron, the director of the 2009 movie *Avatar*, should film his next blockbuster on Ieodo because the *Avatar* script told the story 'of a plucky indigenous people whose home is threatened by a militarily superior and morally corrupt force' ("International Conference to be Held", 23/06/2011). The SIR had also sought to emphasize the strengths of South Korea's claims by holding its first ever one-day international conference in late June 2011 under the banner of 'Maritime Boundary Disputes in East China Sea: Ieodo'. The conference was sponsored by the *Korea Times* (Kim Se-jeong, 30/06/2011). At the defense level, Seoul arguably sought to demonstrate its resolve and capabilities a number of months after the salvage incident when it announced that its Coast Guard would be conducting emergency exercises near the submerged feature and within South Korea's EEZ in early September 2011 ("Coast guard conducts emergency exercise", 06/09/2011). By December 2011, Beijing declared its intention to dispatch a maritime monitoring vessel to the waters close to Socotra Rock for the purpose of displaying its jurisdictional rights in the area (Song Sang-ho, 12/03/2012).

China's Mixed Signals

Tensions over Socotra Rock flared up again in early March 2012. The controversy on this occasion related to remarks made by the Director of the PRC's SOA, Liu Cigui (also *Xigui*). In a March interview with the Xinhua News Agency, Liu told reporters that the SOA had launched a monitoring system of surveillance ships and aircraft intended for the waters surrounding Socotra Rock (Chang Jae-Soon, 12/03/2012). Liu stated that the feature was located within the PRC's 'jurisdictional waters' and as such it was permissible for PRC vessels to patrol the area. Indeed, Liu commented that they would enforce PRC law in the area and step up the frequency of their patrols. China's Foreign Ministry spokesperson Liu Weimin also asserted that jurisdiction of the feature had yet to be decided by the two neighbors and 'before that, neither side should undertake any unilateral activity in the area' (Page, 14/03/2012).

Reports of the interview also noted that the Director had mentioned patrolling by ships and planes, and the enforcement of Chinese domestic law in all areas under PRC jurisdiction 'including Ieodo' (Song Sang-ho, 12/03/2012). Such a declaration by a high-ranking Chinese official bore similarities to the previously mentioned 2008 website controversy and caused a stir among South Korean citizens and the country's media when the story became public (Kang Hyun-kyung, 12/03/2012). The following week, the ROK's Ministry of Foreign Affairs and Trade summoned the PRC's ambassador to South Korea, Zhang Xinsen, to meet with a senior official who protested against Liu's remarks. He also sought an explanation for the statement as well as an official clarification of Beijing's position following the news story. Speaking on the condition of anonymity, a Foreign Ministry official informed reporters afterward that Seoul had expressed in unequivocal terms the South Korean position that China's claims to the feature were unacceptable and that it was and would remain within the ROK's maritime territory. Seoul also demanded that the Chinese drop their claims. According to an article in the *Korea Times*, Beijing later accepted Seoul's demands (Kang Hyun-kyung, 12/03/2012). The article did not expand upon this last assertion. Another source cites the ROK's Deputy Foreign Minister Kim Jae-shin as telling PRC Ambassador Zhang Xinsen 'we cannot accept any attempt by China to formally exercise jurisdictional control' ("Korea Seeks Fresh Negotiations", 13/03/2012). In an ROK press briefing on 15 March 2012, the spokesperson and Deputy Minister for Public Relations, Cho Byung-jae, responded to a question about the March SOA claim controversy by stating, 'China said that the remarks by the director of China's State Oceanic Administration on March 3 were made "just" to explain technical matters, not to strengthen China's position on this issue or to express a particular political intention' (ROK Ministry of Foreign Affairs, 15/03/2012).

Reflecting South Korea's strong desire to not allow the Ieodo issue to damage the wider relationship prior to the 20th anniversary of diplomatic relations in August 2012, as well as to calm domestic anxieties over the issue, ROK President Lee Myung-bak sought to outline his government's position. He chose to do this by publicly participating in a forum hosted by the Korea News Editors' Association. This forum included the editors from the country's leading newspapers and broadcasting companies. During the event, Lee declared that 'it is a matter of course that the rock outcropping of Ieodo off South Korea's southern island of Jeju will remain under Seoul's control in the future' (Chang Jae-Soon, 12/03/2012; Song Sang-ho, 12/03/2012). He also emphasized that the country's position was strong on the basis of the feature being 80.45 nmi from the ROK's southernmost island, Marado, whereas Beijing's claims could not stand up to scrutiny because the nearest PRC territory, Dongdao, is 133.3 nmi away from the submerged rock. This reality, he argued, naturally meant that South Korea would also be at a considerable advantage in any future negotiations on overlapping EEZs. As it stood, the two countries had already attempted to resolve the issue during 16 rounds of EEZ talks, but with no tangible result ("S. Korea Disputes", 12/03/2012; Song Sang-ho, 12/03/2012; Chang Jae-Soon, 12/03/2012). Be that as it may, the President expressed his belief that the feature was unquestionably a part of the country's maritime territory. This was reflected in Lee's comment:

> I want to say that whatever form it may take, Ieodo comes within South Korea's jurisdiction.

He also stressed the sensitivity and importance of Ieodo and its adjacent waters to the South Korean economy by further stating:

> How we manage the waters near Jeju is closely related to South Korea's economy. Thus [we] cannot help but respond sensitively to this issue. (Song Sang-ho, 12/03/2012)

In addition, the South Korean leader warned, 'should a certain type of dispute occur near the waters off Jeju Island, this will give a serious blow to our economy'. Alongside the domestic political benefits of assertively defending the ROK's claim, another indirect effect of the forum and Lee's comments was that they put further pressure on Beijing to concede to

Seoul's position on the issue (Kang Hyun-kyung, 12/03/2012). However, Lee also used the occasion to downplay the controversy surrounding Liu's comments and to emphasize the positive side of Sino-Korean relations. To this end, he reminded the attendees, 'First of all, we have to understand that the Ieodo issue is not a territorial matter ... because it is 4–5 meters under the sea surface' and that dialogue with Beijing was 'going fairly well'. He likewise asserted that despite occasional tensions, Sino-Korean relations were in good shape. This was reflected by the importance which the Chinese leadership placed on ties with Seoul and to the fact that Lee had held more summit meetings (nine in four years) with the PRC President than any of his predecessors. Lee also praised China's attempts at securing peace and stability on the divided peninsula, and stated how the widespread view that the PRC favored North Korea over South Korea in all affairs was unfounded and an oversimplification of what actually happens (Chang Jae-Soon, 12/03/2012).

An international forum centered on the Socotra Rock issue was held in Taipei, Taiwan, in mid-September 2012. The event was co-hosted by the *Korea Times*, the Society of Ieodo Research, and the Taiwanese Academia Sinica. The motivations given for holding the forum were concerns over China's naval activities as well as the natural resources of the East China Sea. Kang Byeong-Cheol, cited elsewhere in this work and a Society of Ieodo Research scholar, declared in an interview prior to the forum, 'It is of great strategic interest considering China's strengthening naval power because China is a powerful country, Korea must look after the interests of its exclusive economic zone (EEZ)' (Kim Young-Jin, 18/09/2012). In this period, Chinese academics such as Zhao Jianming also emphasized the need for Beijing to be tough and resolute in defending PRC claims. In a *Global Times* article titled 'Cautious but firm attitude needed over Suyan Rock dispute with S. Korea', he declared:

> In the future, China should attach more attention to this issue. China should strength [sic] the coordination between its marine patrols and diplomatic measures, using these methods to oppose South Korea's unilateral actions and infringement of Chinese sovereignty. It should force South Korea to get back to the negotiating table. ... China should also establish mechanisms to keep an eye on South Korea and prevent it from making an issue of Hupijiao Rock and Yajiao Rock which are located near Suyan Rock and in the Yellow Sea and the East China Sea. (Zhao Jianming, 14/11/2012)

As with similar incidents which have increased in frequency since 2003, the March 2012 event reflected the delicate balancing act which both states must perform for the benefit of its domestic audience, as well as its rivalry for Socotra Rock. It also shows how relations vis-à-vis Socotra Rock can fluctuate from positive to negative and vice versa within relatively short time periods. During President Park Geun-hye's[7] term, for example, bilateral relations markedly improved,[8] but Socotra Rock-related tensions still threatened to upset ties. Early June 2013 saw the two neighbors commit to intensifying efforts to conclude a Free Trade Agreement (FTA).[9] Park's first Korea-China summit (in Beijing) in late June of that same year produced a joint communiqué where Beijing and Seoul committed themselves to enhancing their ties in numerous areas, including fisheries, and to cooperating on security issues, most notably the denuclearization of the Korean Peninsula ("President Park holds 1st", 28/06/2013). The two leaders also committed themselves to making the Yellow Sea 'a sea of peaceful cooperation and friendship' ("S. Korea-China maritime border", 23/12/2015). Park's removal from office in the midst of a scandal investigation in March 2017 had no tangible impact on the Socotra Rock dispute, although the affair reminded observers of the fragility and vagaries of domestic politics in the ROK and the difficulties associated with maintaining a stable bilateral approach to this issue. One additional difficulty in maintaining this stability involved China's controversial declaration of their Air Defense Identification Zone (ADIZ) in late 2013. South Korea's careful balancing act involved reasserting its jurisdiction and sovereignty while avoiding escalation, a remarkable effort expanded on in the next chapter.

Notes

1. Upon ratification in 1996, the PRC added reservations regarding further consultation on maritime jurisdiction and advance approval on the passage of warships. Several months later they also formally declared their rejection of UNCLOS Part XV, Section 2 regarding procedures for binding decisions: http://www.un.org/depts/los/convention_agreements/convention_declarations.htm#China%20Upon%20ratification.
2. In April 2006, the ROK made their own related reservations regarding Part XV, Section 2: https://treaties.un.org/Pages/ViewDetails.aspx?src=TREATY&mtdsg_no=XXI-6-a&chapter=21&clang=_en; http://www.un.org/depts/los/convention_agreements/convention_declarations.htm#RepKorea%20after%20ratification.

3. Precisely, the dates were 7 June 1996 and 29 January 1996.
4. Known as the Korean Institute of Ocean Science and Technology (KIOST) as of July 2012; http://www.kiost.ac.kr/eng/sub01_02.do.
5. According to the Korea Hydrographic and Oceanographic Administration (KHOA) website, it would appear that the erstwhile Central Committee on Geographical Names fell under the authority of the National Geographic Information Institute. Following this, the Korea Committee on Marine Geographical Names (KCMGN) was established on 1 July 2002; see http://eng.khoa.go.kr/kcom/cnt/selectContentsPage.do?cntId=21060000.
6. The Ministry reverted to its previous name 'Ministry of Foreign Affairs' (MOFA) in 2013.
7. On 10 March 2017, Park was removed from her office as President of the Republic of Korea following a corruption scandal; for more details, see https://www.nytimes.com/2017/03/30/world/asia/park-geun-hye-south-korea-arrest.html.
8. For an interesting article on President Park Guen-hye's China Policy, see Jaeho Kwang, 'The ROK's China Policy Under Park Geun-hye: A New Model of ROK-PRC Relations', Center for East Asian Policy Studies, Brookings Institution, August 2014 at http://www.brookings.edu/~/media/research/files/papers/2014/08/south-korea-china-policy-hwang/south-korea-china-policy-hwang-working-paper.
9. The two sides signed the FTA on 1 June 2015. Xi and Park, respectively, referred to the pact as an 'historic milestone' in their 'efforts to deepen their strategic cooperative partnership'. See http://thediplomat.com/2015/06/its-official-china-south-korea-sign-free-trade-agreement/; China FTA Network, 02/06/2015, http://fta.mofcom.gov.cn/english/.

Bibliography

Chang, Jae-soon. "Lee: Ieodo will remain under Korea's control", (12/03/2012), *Korea Times*. http://www.koreatimes.co.kr/www/news/nation/2012/03/116_106770.html

Chin, Haeng-Nam. "Conflict over the reef's jurisdiction continues to cast a shadow over Korean and Chinese relations." *Jeju Weekly*, 03/02/2014. http://www.jejuweekly.com/news/articleView.html?idxno=3848

China Chafes at Korean Observatory on Reef Island (14/09/2006), *Chosun Ilbo*. http://english.chosun.com/site/data/html_dir/2006/09/14/2006091461017.html

China demands S. Korea stop hoisting sunken ship near Ieodo (27/07/2011), *Yonhap News Agency*. http://english.yonhapnews.co.kr/national/2011/07/27/19/0301000000AEN20110727006300315F.html

China disputes S. Korea's ownership of Ieo Island (14/09/2006), *Hankyoreh*. http://english.hani.co.kr/arti/english_edition/e_international/157139.html

China sent gov't vessel to claim Korea's Ieo Island (27/07/2011), *Dong-A Ilbo*. http://english.donga.com/srv/service.php3?biid=2011072774718

Choi, Yearn-hong. 'Ieodo.' *Korea Times*, 25/06/2010. http://www.koreatimes.co.kr/www/news/opinon/2011/04/137_68269.html

Coast guard conducts emergency exercise near Ieodo (06/09/2011), *Yonhap News Agency*. http://english.yonhapnews.co.kr/news/2011/09/06/0200000000AEN20110906008800320.html

Do, Jae-ha. "'One Ocean Forum' Proposed for Maritime Disputes in East Asia." *Korea Times*, 28/09/2014. http://www.koreatimes.co.kr/www/nation/2017/04/356_165367.html

Drifte, Reinhard. "North East Asia: Territorial Disputes and Divided Countries." Seminar Series 2009 at *Daiwa Foundation Japan House*, London, UK. (18/03/2009). http://www.dajf.org.uk/wp-content/uploads/Prof-Driftes-Presentation.pdf

Han, Jane. "Ocean Research Center Built for Climate Change" (13/10/2009), *Korea Times*. http://www.koreatimes.co.kr/www/news/biz/2009/10/123_53490.html

International Conference to be Held on Korean Island of Ieodo (23/06/2011), *Dokdo Times*. http://dokdotimes.blogspot.com/2011/06/international-conference-to-be-held-on.html

Jung, Sung-ki. "S. Korea to Ask China to Rectify Claim Over Ieodo." *Korea Times*, 08/08/2008. http://www.koreatimes.co.kr/www/news/nation/2011/04/205_29027.html

Kang, Byeong-Cheol. "Ieodo, Okinotorishima and International Politics," Society of Ieodo Research (2012).

Kang, Hyun-kyung. "Ieodo protector sparks imagination of Jeju islanders." *Korea Times*, 12/10/2010. http://www.koreatimes.co.kr/www/news/nation/2016/06/113_77786.html

Kang, Hyun-kyung. "Lee says Ieodo not territorial dispute." *Korea Times*, 12/03/2012. http://www.koreatimes.co.kr/www/news/nation/2012/03/116_106794.html

Kim, Se-jeong. "Ieodo seminar explores Korea's new frontier." *Korea Times*, 30/06/2011. http://www.koreatimes.co.kr/www/news/nation/2012/02/359_89975.html

Kim, Young-jin. "Why Ieodo matters." *Korea Times*, 18/09/2012. http://www.koreatimes.co.kr/www/news/nation/2012/09/117_120266.html

Korea Hydrographic and Oceanographic Agency. "Ieodo." 2010. http://eng.khoa.go.kr/kcom/cnt/selectContentsPage.do?cntId=ieodo_submain

Korea Seeks Fresh Negotiations Over Submerged Rocks (13/03/2012), *Chosun Ilbo*. http://english.chosun.com/site/data/html_dir/2012/03/13/2012031300849.html

Military holds course on Jeju naval base (08/03/2012), *Korea Herald*. http://www.koreaherald.com/view.php?ud=20120308001136&ACE_SEARCH=1

Page, Jeremy. "China, South Korea in Row Over Submerged Rock." *Wall Street Journal*, 13/03/2012. http://blogs.wsj.com/chinarealtime/2012/03/13/china-south-korea-in-row-over-submerged-rock/

PRC Foreign Ministry. Press Conference, 14/09/2006. http://www.fmprc.gov.cn/eng/xwfw/s2510/t272110.htm

PRC State Oceanic Administration. 2014. http://english.gov.cn/state_council/2014/10/06/content_281474992889983.htm

President Park holds 1st Korea-China summit in Beijing (28/06/2013), *Korea Net*. http://www.korea.net/NewsFocus/Policies/view?articleId=109560

ROK Ministry of Foreign Affairs. Press Briefing, 15/03/2012.

S. Korea-China maritime border should be drawn at halfway point (23/12/2015), *Donga Ilbo*. http://english.donga.com/List/3/all/26/411940/1

S. Korea Disputes China's Claim Over Ieodo Rocks (12/03/2012), *RTT News*. http://www.rttnews.com/1838718/s-korea-disputes-china-s-claim-over-ieodo-rocks.aspx

Shin, Hae-in. "China demanded S. Korea stop activities near Ieodo." *Korea Herald*, 27/07/2011. http://www.koreaherald.com/national/Detail.jsp?newsMLId=20110727000696

Snyder, Scott. "China-Korea Relations: Teenage Angst: 15th Anniversary of Diplomatic Relations." *Comparative Connections* (October 2007). http://cc.csis.org/2007/10/teenage-angst-15th-anniversary-diplomatic-relations/

Song, Sang-ho. "Ieodo not part of territorial dispute with China: Lee." Korea Herald, 12/03/2012. http://www.koreaherald.com/national/Detail.jsp?newsMLId=20120312001239

Song, Yann-huei. "Submerged Geographical Features in the East and South China Seas: An Analysis of the Chinese Claims from the Perspective of the Law of the Sea." Ieodo Journal 2 (2012).

Surhone, Lambert M., Mariam T. Tennoe and Susan F. Henssonow, eds. *Socotra Rock – Reef, Territorial Dispute, Exclusive Economic Zone, Marado, Jeju-do.* Beau Bassin, Mauritius: VDM Publishing, 2010.

Van Dyke, Jon M. "Ieodo." Maritime Boundary Disputes in the East China Sea (conference), Yonsei University, Seoul, South Korea, 30/06/2011–01/07/2011.

Wang, Manna. "South Korea and China Conflict Over Islet in East China Sea." *Epoch Times*, 26/08/2007. https://www.theepochtimes.com/south-korea-and-china-conflict-over-islet-in-east-china-sea_1732773.html

Zhao, Jianming. "Cautious but firm attitude needed over Suyan Rock dispute with S. Korea." *Global Times*, 11/14/2012. http://www.globaltimes.cn/content/744314.shtml

CHAPTER 5

Balancing Act: China's Air Defense Declaration

Abstract Here, the significance of China's controversial and somewhat overlooked Air Defense Identification Zone (ADIZ) declaration in November 2013 is examined in general and then specific to the Socotra Rock dispute. The move incorporated the airspace over the submerged feature and included identification rules that aircraft entering the unilaterally declared zone would have to obey. The new ADIZ overlapped with both South Korea's and Japan's own respective ADIZs. This spurred South Korea to conduct military activities, some of them including Japan, aimed at publicly rejecting the new ADIZ while also instructing airlines to ignore it. One leading scholar opined at the time that the situation could become 'extremely dangerous' if the PRC ever decided to intercept non-complying aircraft. On the domestic front in South Korea, a key consequence was that the declaration caused many people to better comprehend and appreciate the strategic importance of the area in which Socotra Rock is located.

Keywords Air Defense Identification Zone (ADIZ) • South Korean military activities

The significance of China's controversial and somewhat overlooked Air Defense Identification Zone (ADIZ) declaration in November 2013 merits some general examination as well as how it relates to the Socotra Rock dispute. The declaration incorporated the airspace over the submerged

S. Fox, *China, South Korea, and the Socotra Rock Dispute*,
https://doi.org/10.1007/978-981-13-2077-4_5

feature and included identification rules that aircraft entering the unilaterally declared zone would have to obey. Remarkably, this new ADIZ overlapped both South Korea's and Japan's own respective ADIZs. This spurred South Korea to conduct military activities, some of them including Japan, aimed at publicly rejecting the new ADIZ while also instructing airlines to ignore it. Leading scholars and analysts expressed concern at the time that the situation had the potential to become perilous if the PRC ever decided to intercept non-complying aircraft. On South Korea's domestic front, a key consequence was that the declaration caused many people to better comprehend and appreciate the strategic importance of Socotra Rock's location. Seoul reacted to Beijing's move by expanding the Korean ADIZ (KADIZ) a month later. Following that, a state-sponsored PRC newspaper reacted to the move by issuing a warning to Seoul about the consequences of drifting away from their existing ties and then pointed an accusing finger at Japan (Chao Lü, 19/12/2013).

This gave rise to varying perspectives that viewed the move as a harmless but effective gesture, one aimed primarily at Japan, that allowed China to assert sovereignty over a wide area of the East China Sea, to more sinister interpretations of the ADIZ claim. Korean observers interpreted the act as part and parcel of Beijing's rejection of the ROK's jurisdictional rights in maritime areas to its west and south. In their view, China's new ADIZ appeared to undermine a tacit bilateral understanding as well as frequently cited assurances by Beijing that the Socotra Rock issue was not about sovereignty. In addition, the use of the word 'defense' confused ROK citizens and security analysts alike and prompted calls for a reassessment of the threat posed by China in adjacent waters (Shin Hyon-hee, 08/06/2015). Despite foreseeable disruptions in ties, Seoul notably was careful to reassert its jurisdiction over the waters and airspace around Socotra Rock while taking care, where possible, to not unnecessarily raise tensions with Beijing over the issue.

China's Declaration

It was on 23 November 2013 that the PRC controversially declared an ADIZ in the East China Sea, which incorporated the airspace over Socotra Rock. The declaration stipulated a number of identification rules that aircraft entering the unilaterally declared zone would have to follow. These included the demand that both civilian and military aircraft identify themselves to either the PRC's Foreign Ministry or the PRC's Civil Aviation

Administration and provide flight plan, radio, transponder, and logo details. Commenting shortly after the declaration, the American scholar Victor Cha cautioned that due to the fact that many aircraft from countries such as Japan, for example, will choose to ignore the ADIZ, the situation could become 'extremely dangerous' if the PRC ever decided to intercept non-compliant aircraft (Cha, 2013: 2) (Maps 5.1 and 5.2).[1]

There is an overlap between a large area of Japan's own air defense identification zone (JADIZ) and a smaller strip of the KADIZ south of Jeju Island. South Korea's pre-December 2013 zone had been drawn up by the US military in 1951 (Gale and Lee, 08/12/2013). Japan designated its current air defense zone in 1969, revising it following Okinawa's reversion to Japanese sovereignty in 1972. It was revised again, this time

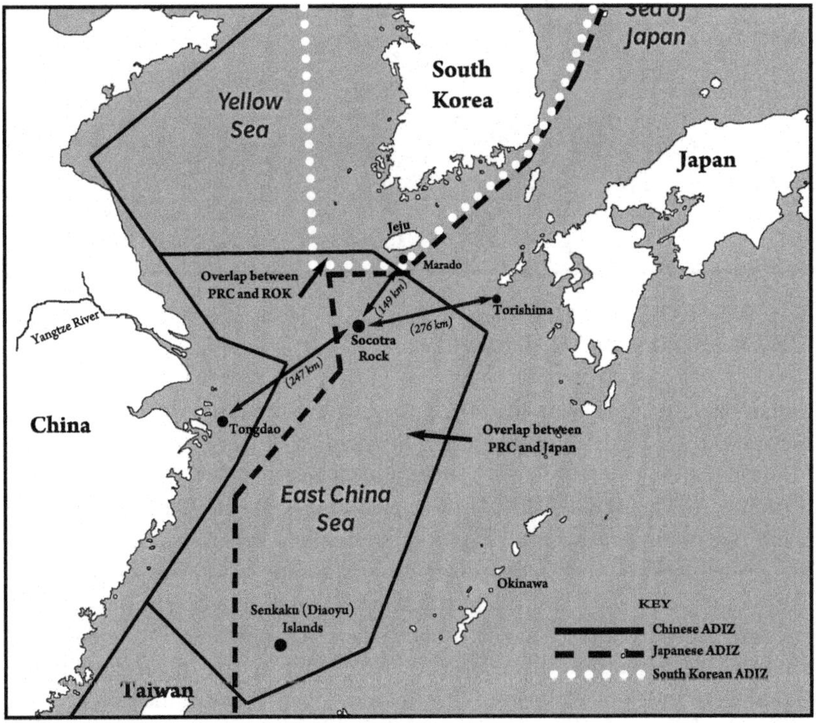

Map 5.1 ADIZs for China, South Korea, and Japan before the South Korean ADIZ was extended in December 2013

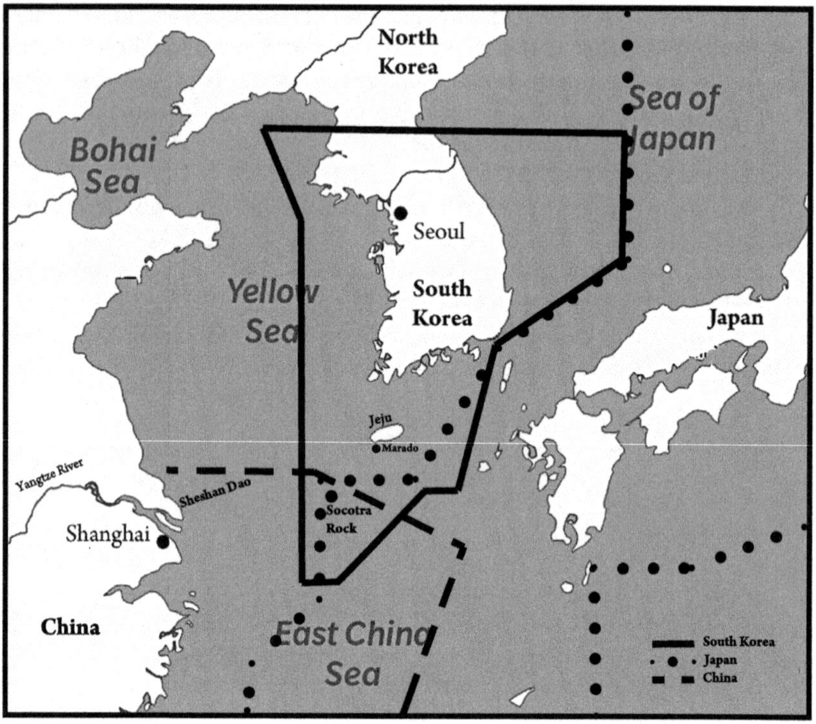

Map 5.2 ADIZs for China, South Korea, and Japan after the South Korean ADIZ was extended in December 2013

unilaterally, on 26 June 2010, westward by 22 km and overlapping Taiwan's own ADIZ. Interestingly, Socotra Rock then was found to be inside Japan's air defense zone, although Japan has never claimed jurisdiction over it. The new KADIZ was unproblematic for the Japanese because it did not incorporate airspace over Japanese land territory (excluding the Liancourt Rocks) and because an understanding was reached between Tokyo and Seoul with no ramifications for the free movement of commercial activities. Hikariko Ono, a spokesperson for Japanese Prime Minister Shinzo Abe, noted that this was in contrast to the actions taken by Beijing, which were in contravention of international norms and standards according to the ROK-USA-Japan perspective. It has also been noted by a senior Korean scholar, Yang Uk, that the zone's expansion had no discernible influence on the Socotra Rock issue (Gale and Lee, 08/12/2013).

According to Hsu, however, a central motivation for Beijing's declaration of an ADIZ was that 'an ADIZ allows China greater flexibility in asserting sovereignty over its ECS claims in a manner that does not controvert international conventions' (Hsu, 2014: 1). While it appears that the Chinese aimed the move at Japan in relation to Sino-Japanese disagreements over the East China Sea, Korean observers interpreted the act as part and parcel of Beijing's rejection of the ROK's jurisdictional rights in the Yellow Sea and northern East China Sea areas. At the official level, the PRC attempted to allay South Korean concerns about the new ADIZ in late November 2013 by stating in bilateral defense talks that the move was aimed at Tokyo and not Seoul (Keck, 02/12/2013).

On 25 November 2013, PRC Foreign Ministry spokesperson Qin Gang, when questioned about the PRC's new ADIZ, stated 'the ROK and China have no territorial dispute' and that 'the two sides will solve the issue through friendly consultations and negotiations'. He also claimed 'I also want to point out that China and the ROK are friendly neighbors. We hope, on this issue, that we can win coordination and understanding from the ROK side' (Kim Ji-hyun, 25/11/2013).

South Korea Reacts

South Korea nevertheless defied China's new ADIZ by flying a reconnaissance plane close to Socotra Rock on 26 November without notifying Beijing in advance (Pedrozo, 2014: 71). And less than a week later, on 2 December, a DDG 992 Aegis class destroyer, the *Yulgok Yi* I, was mobilized from South Korea's largest naval base, Jinhae (Chinhae), sailing 17 hours to the feature and anchoring just 200 meters from the research station in advance of a joint air and sea military exercise. The exercise was conducted by the ROKN the following day. The drill also involved the dispatch of two P-3 anti-submarine planes and involved monitoring the IORS as well as its surrounding waters. A senior public relations officer for the ROKN informed the media that 'Under international law, Ieodo is located in open waters, but because of our maritime research station, it is pretty much our territory', and that 'this operation is our Navy's way of showing its intention to protect our jurisdiction over Ieodo's waters' (Jeong & Kim, 04/12/2013; Keck, 04/12/2013).

It is worth noting that the South Koreans provided advance notice to Japan before flying the two P-3 planes through the part of their flight plan that included the Japanese ADIZ. This was at a time when Seoul was advising ROK airlines to ignore the stipulations attached to recognizing China's air defense identification zone (Jeong & Kim, 04/12/2013; Keck, 04/12/2013). The 3 December exercise was followed on 12 December by a joint ROKN-Japanese Maritime Self-Defense Force (JMSDF) search and research (SAR) exercise inside the Chinese ADIZ. The drill included the use of at least one helicopter and ignored the new air defense zone ("Japan, S. Korea Hold Joint Sea", 12/12/2013).

According to Shin, on the domestic front in South Korea, China's ADIZ declaration had two main consequences. One was that South Koreans, long accustomed to occasional skirmishes with North Korea along the Northern Limit Line (NLL) in the Yellow Sea, reached a greater appreciation of the strategic importance of the East China Sea area in which Socotra Rock is located. The second was the embarrassing realization that the feature was in fact situated within Japan's ADIZ (JADIZ) (Shin Hyon-hee, 08/06/2015). This resulted in Seoul taking measures to extend South Korea's ADIZ on 15 December 2013. The official PRC news agency, *Xinhua News*, ran a story in advance on 10 December declaring that Beijing had expressed regret over the ROK's decision and hoped that the South Koreans could manage the issue well ("China expresses regret", 10/12/2013). Two *Global Times* articles reacted just before and after Seoul's official ADIZ declaration by commenting 'South Korea's nationalism, which is different from Japan's, poses no threat to China. South Korea needs to be wary of the serious results if it drifts away from healthy China-South Korea ties' ("Seoul takes Petty Advantage", 09/12/2013). It subsequently pointed the finger at Japan for sowing discord between the two neighbors: 'the intention of a certain state to play Seoul against Beijing will not succeed' (Chao Lü, 19/12/2013).

South Korea's ADIZ expansion on 15 December saw its ADIZ increase by about 103,600 square kilometers and included Socotra Rock (Kuo, 09/12/2013). ROK officials such as the Director General for Public Planning at the state's Ministry of Defense, Jang Hyuk, stated during a December 2013 press conference that the extended ADIZ was drawn up to make it more compatible with their country's civilian airlines-related Flight Information Region (FIR), which is designated by the International Civil Aviation Organization (ICAO). He stated, 'As the FIR covers the airspace over Ieodo (Suyan Rock) and Hongdo and Marado, the government has decided to match the KADIZ with the FIR' (Zhang, 09/12/2013).

It was the first time that the ROK expanded its ADIZ in 62 years since the USA had first designated it in 1951, and surprisingly, the first time that the KADIZ incorporated Socotra Rock (Shin Hyon-hee, 08/06/2015). Despite foreseeable disruptions in ties, it was interesting to note Seoul's actions to reassert its jurisdiction over the waters and airspace around Socotra Rock while taking care not to unnecessarily raise tensions with Beijing over the issue. A notable example was the failure of the Jeju Special Self-Governing Provincial Council to win legal governmental approval from Seoul for the establishment of an 'Ieodo Day' in December 2013. The proposal had also failed in 2007, 2008, and 2012 (Chin, 03/02/2014).

Commitment to Resolve

A bilateral summit in July 2014 saw South Korean President Park Geun-hye and Chinese President Xi Jinping commit to restarting official negotiations aimed at resolving the dispute. Their commitment was to commence talks in 2015, and their resolve was reflected in the decision to place the working-level group talks in the hands of vice-ministerial level negotiators after years at the director-general level ("S. Korea-China maritime border", 23/12/2015). It also marked the first time that the two countries would engage in formal negotiations toward an agreed demarcation line (Tiezzi, 07/11/2015). To this end, on 29 January 2015, the first meeting addressed the questions of EEZs and continental shelves (Yoon, 2015: 1).

In March 2015, on the security front and as part of wider maritime strategic maneuvers, the joint exercises 'Foal Eagle' and 'Key Resolve' began in late February. Here, the USA and South Korean navies conducted a drill in which, among other exercises, they practiced defending the feature. An ROK naval officer stated at the time that they would use the drill to practice helicopter departures and landings by Lynx anti-submarine helicopters from the helipad on the IORS and that South Korean Coastguard units from Jeju Island would also be involved in the exercises. These were backed up by a South Korean destroyer *Ganggamchan*, P-3 C patrol aircraft, a Coastguard Kamov helicopter, and other ships while US warships, destroyers, and helicopters rehearsed related maneuvers in nearby waters (Jun Ji-hye, 01/03/2015). In July 2015, Seoul commissioned the Airbus A330 MRTT, the world's largest aerial refueling tanker. The move was aimed at maximizing the response effectiveness of surveillance flights over Socotra Rock as well as the

Liancourt Rocks while also extending the available overhead flight time above the feature from 20 minutes to 80 minutes (Arirang, 02/07/2015).

During his sideline summit with ROK President Park on 31 October, and just prior to the sixth China-Japan-South Korea Trilateral Summit in Seoul on 1 November 2015, Chinese Premier Li Keqiang proposed a speedy recommencement of official maritime demarcation talks (Song, 02/11/2015; 21/12/2015). This proposal was also confirmed by Chinese media outlets ("Repeated Follies", 05/11/2015).[2] When the sidelines summit concluded, the Chinese Foreign Ministry published their proposal in a press release on its website, and at a press conference on 6 November, PRC Foreign Ministry spokesperson Hua Chunying stated, 'it is hoped that China and the ROK can fairly and properly resolve the overlapping claims of maritime rights and interests through amicable consultations and set a good example for regional countries in addressing similar issues'. She also said that both countries agreed that the first round of talks would take place in December, and declared that the main purpose of the talks was 'to fairly and properly demarcate the China-ROK maritime boundary through negotiations and consultations' and that it was 'of great significance to upholding tranquility and stability of the relevant waters and consolidating and growing bilateral friendly cooperation'. Hua continued by declaring that the talks would give 'full expression to China's long-standing stance and position to settle maritime disputes with its neighbors through bilateral dialogues on the basis of respecting historical facts and international law' (PRC Foreign Ministry, 06/11/2015). The plan to recommence talks had been confirmed by ROK Foreign Ministry Deputy Spokesperson Sun Nahm-kook on 5 November when he told waiting reporters that 'the two countries have been holding relevant discussions and are working to set the date of the first meeting for some time in December 2015' (ROK Ministry of Foreign Affairs, Press Briefing 05/11/2015).

One observer noted the timing of the Chinese proposal on 31 October, with the South Koreans facing pressure to declare their position on the PRC's activities in the South China Sea. These activities involved China often converting submerged rocks and reefs into artificial islands, which then could be used for military purposes (Song, 02/11/2015). In the period leading up to the November 2015 summit, China experienced some setbacks in terms of its claims in the South China Sea. In one case, during a Freedom of Navigation Operation (FONOP), the USS *Frasen*, a guided missile destroyer, defended a central plank of US principles in the

South China Sea, specifically 'freedom of navigation' by sailing within 12 nmi of a PRC-controlled feature in the area, Subi Reef (Tiezzi, 07/11/2015). In another case, the Permanent Court of Arbitration (PCA) in the Hague determined that its jurisdictional remit extended to judging the Philippines' protests against China's claims in the South China Sea. Beijing protested this decision to no avail (Tiezzi, 07/11/2015). It is thus perhaps not coincidental that China viewed South Korea as its 'best bet', according to Shannon Tiezzi, in terms of presenting a 'good example' of how a state should address a maritime dispute with China. First, if maritime talks with the ROK proceed smoothly, then the Chinese could show other states with which it has a dispute that China can resolve disagreements 'peacefully and equitably'. This could possibly improve China's reputation vis-à-vis disputes in the East China Sea and the South China Sea. Another possible benefit of an agreed demarcation line with South Korea was that it could be promoted as evidence of the 'right' approach to resolving problems with the PRC, specifically through bilateral talks. An agreed delimitation could be held up against other approaches such as letting an international tribunal apply international legal standards to resolving the dispute or asking the regional Association of South East Asian Nations (ASEAN) to pressure a resolution on disputants via collective multi-national action. Tiezzi goes on to argue that these benefits for China could possibly convince Beijing to agree to a resolution in which Seoul appears to have gained more than lost so as to show how bilateral talks with the PRC can be both 'productive and profitable' (Tiezzi, 07/11/2015).

Stratfor likewise held a similar view on the possibilities of, and motivations for, China making concessions in the maritime negotiations. These include drawing the ROK closer to China; weakening the USA-South Korea-Japan alliance structure by undermining US influence in East Asia; encouraging bilateral talks between China and other states with which it has maritime disputes; and disincentivizing South Korean involvement in the South China Sea disputes. All of the above run counter to Washington's objectives in the region ("Why China Would Compromise", 10/12/2015). Other observers also expressed optimism concerning China's likely approach since late 2015. Kor Kian Beng, China Bureau Chief at the *Straits Times*, for example, points to a number of interviewed analysts. Some of them believe that the Chinese are hoping to use a constructive approach with South Korea to make progress with its wider geopolitical aims, such as in regards to its territorial claims in the South China Sea. Dr. Yu Yingli, a China-Korea expert at the Shanghai Institute of International Affairs, observes how bilateral ties did at one point improve significantly from late 2012 under the PRC's President Xi Jinping and South Korean President Park Geun-hye. This was symbolized by a free trade agreement in June 2015, though since then there have been new tensions, with the Socotra Rock issue representing a lingering sore in the relationship. As Yu contends, 'Issues of national sovereignty are always sensitive. Both sides may deem that it is better to resolve this than to let it become a potential ticking time bomb' (Kor, 16/12/2015). As discussed later, however, a number of other scholars challenge such perspectives.

Other experts such as Song Sang-ho predicted that progress would be slow and frustrating, and negotiations protracted due to China's objective of maximizing its access to economically vital energy and maritime resources in the Yellow Sea and the East China Sea. And as argued by international law specialist Kang Hyo-baik, 'China has been focusing on securing more energy and resources thought to be stored in its continental shelf. Thus, it is unlikely to budge from its position' (Song, 21/12/2015). Nanjing University's Zhu Feng was likewise doubtful for two reasons. One was the mutual understanding since 2014 by the leaders of China and South Korea to commence talks. The other was the fact that it was presumptuous to imagine China, like other states, 'would give in easily' in terms of making concessions on issues related to national sovereignty. It was thus too early and too difficult to precisely measure the influence of Yellow Sea EEZ talks on the South China Sea disputes (Kor, 16/12/2015).

Carl Thayer, a regional security expert, likewise emphasized the stark differences between the two disputes and the limitations of the smaller 'more straightforward' Sino-South Korean purely jurisdictional-related dispute over a submerged feature and the much more complicated sovereignty-related South China Sea disagreements. Thayer noted that Southeast Asian states with an interest in the South China Sea disputes would remain skeptical about Beijing's use of bilateral negotiations with Seoul as an example of what bilateral talks could produce, adding 'Given China's construction of artificial islands and its lurking presence in Malaysian waters, China's call for bilateral relations will fall on deaf ears'. An authority on South China Sea disagreements, Ian Storey, was also dismissive of drawing a direct link between the two cases and stated 'While not straightforward, resolving a dispute between two countries is easier than resolving one that involves six parties, like in the South China Sea' (Kor, 16/12/2015).

On 22 December 2015, South Korea and China recommenced Yellow Sea EEZ delimitation talks, their first since 2008. Despite 14 rounds of director-level talks from 1996 until 2008, the two sides had, by 2008, failed to reach a satisfactory conclusion. The high-level December 2015 meeting between the PRC's Vice Foreign Minister Liu Zhenmin and the ROK's Vice Foreign Minister Cho Tae-yul came to naught. The two sides reiterated their positions on key issues, including the median line versus a revised 'fairness principle' line that factors in China's long coastline, greater landmass, larger population, and continental shelf claims ("Seoul-Beijing EEZ talks", 23/12/2015; "S. Korea-China maritime border", 23/12/2015). Another source confirmed that the PRC's negotiators stuck to their position that the dividing line in the Yellow Sea should be drawn further eastward and closer to the Korean coastline due to China's higher population, greater landmass, and longer coastline. Following the meeting, Cho informed the media that talks would continue into the future but cautioned they would be 'difficult and lengthy' (Ryall, 23/12/2015). They did promise, however, to follow up the December 2015 meeting with similar vice-ministerial level talks once a year in conjunction with director general-level meetings ("Seoul-Beijing EEZ talks", 23/12/2015; "S. Korea-China maritime border", 23/12/2015). The background to all of this, however, was also prompted by significant economic factors woven in with immediate and long-term security concerns on all sides, a discussion that follows.

Notes

1. For an interesting article concerning criticism of South Korea's apparent quiet diplomacy and bilateral requests as well as their overall strategy, see Cha, 2013.
2. This article also discussed how Japan was irritated by China's exploitation of issues such as Socotra Rock to enhance China's influence in South Korea at the expense of Japan (such as meeting President Park separately on 31 October 2015); see Korea Herald, 05/11/2015.

Bibliography

Airbus' aerial tankers to extend operation time up to 4 times (2015-07-02) Arirang News. http://arirang.co.kr/news/news view.asp?nseq=181014&sys_lang=Kor

Cha, Victor. "Korea's Mistake on China's ADIZ Controversy." *Center for Strategic and International Studies, Korea Chair Platform*, 2/12/2013. http://csis.org/files/publication/131202_Koreas_Mistake_on_Chinas_ADIZ_Controversy.pdf

Chao, Lü. "Beijing and Seoul gain much more from close relations." *Global Times*, 18/12/2013. http://epaper.globaltimes.cn/2013-12-19/41389.htm

Chin, Haeng-Nam. "Conflict over the reef's jurisdiction continues to cast a shadow over Korean and Chinese relations." *Jeju Weekly*, 03/02/2014. http://www.jejuweekly.com/news/articleView.html?idxno=3848

China expresses regret over S. Korea's move (2013/12/10), *Xinhuanet News*. http://news.xinhuanet.com/english/video/2013-12/10/c_132955189.htm

Gale, Alastair and Min-Jeong Lee. "South Korea Expands Air-Defense Zone: Move Unlikely to Cause Tension as China Has Accepted Plans." *Wall Street Journal*, 08/12/2013. https://www.wsj.com/articles/south-korea-expands-airdefense-zone-1386484430

Hsu, Kimberly. "Air Defense Identification Zone Intended to Provide China Greater Flexibility to Enforce East China Sea Claims." *U.S.-China Economic and Security Review Commission Staff Report*, January 14, 2014. http://www.uscc.gov/sites/default/files/Research/China%20ADIZ%20Staff%20Report.pdf

Japan, S. Korea Hold Joint Sea Drill in China Air Zone (12/12/2013), *Agence France-Presse*. http://www.ndtv.com/world-news/japan-south-korea-hold-joint-sea-drill-in-china-air-zone-544304

Jeong, Yong-Soo and Sarah Kim. "Korean Navy conducts drill close to Ieodo." *Korea JoongAng Daily*, 04/12/2013. http://koreajoongangdaily.joins.com/news/article/article.aspx?aid=2981469

Jun, Ji-hye. "ROK, US Navies to conduct Ieodo defense training today." *Korea Times*, 03/01/2015. http://www.koreatimes.co.kr/www/news/nation/2015/03/116_174348.html

Keck, Zachary. "South Korea Conducts Military Drill in China's ADIZ." *The Diplomat*, 04/12/2013. https://thediplomat.com/2013/12/south-korea-conducts-military-drill-in-chinas-adiz/

Keck, Zachary. "South Korea to Expand Its Air Defense Identification Zone." *The Diplomat*, 02/12/2013. https://thediplomat.com/2013/12/south-korea-to-expand-its-air-defense-identification-zone/

Kim, Ji-hyun. "China informed Seoul of air defense zone." *Korea Herald*, 25/11/2013. http://www.koreaherald.com/view.php?ud=20131125001000

Kor, Kian Beng. "China has wider hopes for Seoul talks, say observers." *Straits Times*, 16/12/2015. http://www.straitstimes.com/asia/east-asia/china-has-wider-hopes-for-seoul-talks-say-observers

Kuo, Lily. "Will a Tiny, Submerged Rock Spark a New Crisis in the East China Sea?" *The Atlantic*, 09/12/2013. http://www.theatlantic.com/china/archive/2013/12/will-a-tiny-submerged-rock-spark-a-new-crisis-in-the-east-china-sea/282155/

Pedrozo, Raul. "The Bull in the China Shop: Raising Tensions in the Asia-Pacific Region," *International Law Studies* 90, no. 66 (2014): 66–100. https://stockton.usnwc.edu/cgi/viewcontent.cgi?article=1049&context=ils

PRC Foreign Ministry. Press Conference, 06/11/2015. http://www.fmprc.gov.cn/mfa_eng/xwfw_665399/s2510_665401/t1312707.shtml

Repeated follies (05/11/2015), *Korea Herald*. http://www.koreaherald.com/view.php?ud=20151105001042

ROK Ministry of Foreign Affairs. Press Briefing, 05/11/2015.

Ryall, Julian. "Beijing lays claim to South Korean waters." *The Telegraph*, 23/12/2015. http://www.telegraph.co.uk/news/worldnews/asia/china/12065626/Beijing-lays-claim-to-South-Korean-waters.html

S. Korea-China maritime border should be drawn at halfway point (23/12/2015), *Donga Ilbo*. http://english.donga.com/List/3/all/26/411940/1

Seoul takes petty advantage but loses big picture (09/12/2013), *Global Times*. http://www.globaltimes.cn/content/831096.shtml

Seoul-Beijing EEZ talks (23/12/2015), *Korea Times*. http://www.koreatimes.co.kr/www/news/opinon/2015/12/202_193883.html

Shin, Hyon-hee. "Seoul seeks to bolster drone use in air defense zone." *Korea Herald*, 08/06/2015. http://www.koreaherald.com/view.php?ud=20150608000932

Song, Sang-ho. "China's proposal for EEZ talks sparks Ieodo concerns." *Korea Herald*, 02/11/2015. http://www.koreaherald.com/view.php?ud=20151102001231

Song, Sang-ho. "Seoul, Beijing hold EEZ talks Tuesday." *Korea Herald*, 21/12/2015. http://www.koreaherald.com/view.php?ud=20151221001084

Tiezzi, Shannon. "It's Official: China, South Korea Sign Free Trade Agreement." *The Diplomat*, 02/06/2015. http://thediplomat.com/2015/06/its-official-china-south-korea-sign-free-trade-agreement/

Tiezzi, Shannon. "Is China Ready to Solve One of Its Maritime Disputes?" *The Diplomat*, 07/11/2015. http://thediplomat.com/2015/11/is-china-ready-to-solve-one-of-its-maritime-disputes/

Why China Would Compromise in the Yellow Sea (10/12/2015), *Stratfor Worldview*. https://www.stratfor.com/analysis/why-china-would-compromise-yellow-sea?utm_source=Twitter&utm_medium=Official&utm_campaign=Link

Yoon, Sukjoon. "Korea-China Maritime Boundary Talks: Implications for South China Sea." *RSIS Commentary* No. 89, 13 April 2015. https://www.rsis.edu.sg/wp-content/uploads/2015/04/CO15089.pdf

Zhang, Yiqian. "Seoul expands KADIZ south." *Global Times*, 09/12/2013. http://www.globaltimes.cn/content/830911.shtml

CHAPTER 6

Recent Economic and Security Factors

Abstract The interrelationship between the Socotra Rock issue and security, domestic political, and economic factors is under scrutiny in this chapter, including how they have tested and continue to test bilateral ties today and in recent years. Since normalization, Sino-South Korean economic ties have witnessed immense growth, from US $6.4 billion in 1992 to a staggering US $220.6 billion in 2011. China's economic footprint in the ROK has alarmed many South Koreans, who fear that their neighbor has a 'superpower mentality' toward the Korean Peninsula. China's economic and political influence upon North Korea in particular has raised serious questions. This sentiment is reflected with regards to Socotra Rock by leading Korean activists. The chapter discusses how such issues are intertwined with 'Ieodo' in South Korean popular and elite perceptions of a growing threat.

Keywords China's economic and political influence • 'Ieodo' • Sino-South Korean economic ties

The relationship between and impact of security and economic factors need to be placed under some scrutiny, especially regarding how they have tested and continue to test bilateral ties today as well as in recent years. As mentioned in a previous chapter, but worth repeating here, is the fact that since normalization in 1992, Sino-South Korean economic ties grew from US $6.4 billion then to an astonishing US $220.6 billion in 2011 and was

S. Fox, *China, South Korea, and the Socotra Rock Dispute*,
https://doi.org/10.1007/978-981-13-2077-4_6

still holding relatively steadily in 2016 at US $211.4 billion (Korea Customs Service, 2018). China's economic footprint in the ROK has alarmed many South Koreans, who fear that their neighbor has a 'superpower mentality' toward the Korean Peninsula.

The economic and political influence of China upon North Korea in particular has also raised serious questions, particularly among leading Korean activists. Importantly, such fears serve to restrict flexibility in negotiations. It similarly suggests how the potentialities of resources near the feature could spur Seoul or Beijing to act more assertively to access them or to deny them to the other side. Fisheries, discussed in Chap. 3, provides just one example of how it can influence China's leverage in agreeing to a revised dividing line: the results of rising demands have included the overfishing of local waters and consequent incursions into neighboring states' EEZs. Core security issues are also worth consideration, including the maintenance of transportation and supply lifelines and the potential of a greater US security presence in the Yellow Sea, notably because it can influence how the two neighbors approach the dispute. How the rise in maritime tensions has coincided with a resurgence of frictions elsewhere between the Chinese and their neighbors also requires some description and analysis. While the PRC has been enhancing its own capabilities in maritime areas since the late 1980s, Chinese military planners have also grown increasingly concerned about how the security connotations of South Korea, as a US ally, has made defense changes and upgrades in recent years, where 'Suyan Jiao' (Socotra Rock) and the neighboring Jeju Island have taken on a greater military significance. This is due in no small part to the construction of the massive Jeju Island naval base. And this in turn undoubtedly influences how Chinese decision-makers perceive South Korean developments around and on the rock. Together, these realities complicate the approaches open to a strategically threatened China in any attempts to resolve this disagreement.

Socotra Rock's Increased Economic Value

While on one hand this dispute has been a cause for concern for the two neighbors, on the other hand policymakers in both states appreciate that their overriding interests lie in further strengthening the unprecedented growth in bilateral trade since the 1990s. However, they also understand that an interminable deadlock in progress and in negotiations on the issue could test the patience of the two countries as they tackle the challenge of feeding economic growth amid increased global competition for energy supplies. Both governments have thus worked hard to ensure that this issue does not escalate into a confrontation from which no one would benefit. As such, the preferred option is to keep the issue on the margins and to agree to disagree in the absence of a resolution. Seoul and Beijing continue to hold firm in terms of their claims and protests. A shared appreciation of where priorities lie has contributed to a calmer approach to the issue than seen in other more historically and politically sensitive disputes such as the East China Sea issue between Japan and China, or more complicated disputes in the South China Sea where numerous players are involved. Nevertheless, while wider economic interests have helped to temper territorial disputes between China and South Korea, the presence of valuable resources as well as speculation about their potential in the area around Socotra Rock could spur Seoul or Beijing to act more assertively to access them or to deny the other side the opportunity to exploit them. Economically and legally, while the feature in question may seem insignificant, the waters in which they sit touch upon key issues for both economies. These include national security, transportation and supply lifelines, and economic resources (Flenniken, 14/08/2011). The *Global Times*, for example, reiterated the import of the 'Suyan Rock' area for China following the ADIZ controversy of November–December 2013 when it stated 'Boasting abundant fishing resources, oil, gas and mineral resources, Suyan Rock is of great significance, apart from its advantageous military position' (Cai, 18/12/2013).

Energy exploration activities have been a constant source of friction between China and Japan in the East China Sea, and between various claimants around the Spratly Islands in the South China Sea. Developments since the early 2000s also suggest that the waters adjacent to Socotra Rock have considerable quantities of hydrocarbons ready to be exploited. A July 2004 *Asia Times* article, for example, reported that surveys had confirmed a large amount of oil resources lay below the seabed of the East China Sea. This, the article argued, provided the South Koreans and the Chinese with an added incentive to be more assertive in defending their conflicting EEZ claims (Flenniken, 14/08/2011). China's *Epoch Times* reported in a 2007 article that 'there are abundant reserves of oil and other minerals at the bottom of the sea' in waters adjacent to 'Suyan Rock' (Wang Manna, 26/08/2007). Korean scholars Yun and Park reported in 2013: 'It is estimated that 7.2 billion tons of natural gas and up to 10 million barrels of crude oil are buried under the entire area of the ECS, including Ieodo' (Yun & Park, 2013: 100).

Notably, Van Dyke comments that even though oil and gas are a 'major issue' in the ongoing maritime disagreements in the East China Sea and the Yellow Sea, the Ieodo Ocean Research Station's website hardly mentions energy resources in nearby waters. It does, however, declare that the rock lies within the maritime territory delineated under South Korea's Maritime Mineral Resource Act of 1970. This legislation stipulates Seoul's submarine mining rights on the sea's continental shelf area without referring specifically to Socotra Rock (Van Dyke, 30/06/2011).

South Korea and particularly China are two countries with a strong national interest in accessing energy resources close to home so as to feed their rising domestic demand for oil and gas and thus maintain economic growth (Flenniken, 14/08/2011). In the one-party PRC, this necessity is all the more pressing for the Chinese Communist Party (CCP), which, since the end of the Cold War, has increasingly depended on the two legitimating objectives of economic prosperity and defending the nation to cement their hold on power amid turbulent domestic change.[1] In this context, and in the absence of any foreseeable agreement on the competing claims, the presence of oil and gas fields or other valuable minerals in the northern East China Sea may tempt decision-makers to take greater risks to access these resources while balancing these activities with the shared desire for enhanced economic ties at the wider bilateral level. Dangerous confrontations elsewhere in East Asia have occurred over lesser issues, so the possibility of trouble over energy exploration near Socotra Rock cannot be ruled out. The increased economic value of the maritime area also arguably provides some compelling reasons as to why Beijing and Seoul have behaved more assertively since 2003 in the process of claim and counter-claim over EEZ rights and activities.

More Pressing Security Concerns

While there are obvious overlaps between economic security issues and military security issues, it is the military and defense component of Sino-South Korean relations which is given more attention here. As the rise in tensions between China and South Korea over the submerged feature coincided with a resurgence of other maritime frictions between China and its neighbors, the worrying discrepancies between what Beijing says and what actually happens suggests it is in Seoul's best interests to hedge its bets regarding the PRC in waters around Socotra Rock. It is also apparent that even though trade relations between South Korea and China exceed that of trade with the USA and Japan combined, conflicting security interests between the two states have often placed greater strains on bilateral ties in recent years. A notable obstacle to the building of trust in the defense field has been Beijing's aforementioned close links with North Korea. As retired Korean naval vice admiral, Yun Yon, explained: 'We may do business with the Chinese, but still it's the Americans we should do security with' (Choe, 19/08/2011).

It is worth noting that the PRC has supported UN-led sanctions against North Korea, with some expressed reservations, following the adoption of UN Security Council (UNSC) Resolution 1718 against the DPRK following a nuclear weapon test on 9 October 2006 (Council on Foreign Relations (CFR), 28/03/2018). When North Korea conducted a missile launch in November 2017, Beijing called on the DPRK to end activities that create heightened tensions and expressed 'grave concern and opposition' (KBS World Radio, 29/11/2017). In comparison to other major powers, however, China's 'punitive steps have been somewhat restrained' with such sanctions often watered down following specific objections by Beijing (Council on Foreign Relations, 28/03/2018). This is in spite of the DPRK's Central Committee of the Workers' Party of Korea allegedly penning a letter in March 2016 that expressed shock at China for agreeing to the sanctions, and calling on North Koreans to confront the PRC with a 'nuclear storm' (Kim Ga Young, 31/03/2016). As observed by Jennifer Lind, an associate professor at Dartmouth College in the USA, 'While the Chinese certainly would prefer that North Korea not have nuclear weapons, their greatest fear is regime collapse' (Lind, 07/08/2017). This apparent support for North Korea at almost all costs no doubt undermines confidence-building initiatives between China and South Korea as they seek to strengthen ties over such issues as Socotra Rock.

Regarding fishing disagreements or where PRC-ROK maritime boundaries should be drawn, the USA has tended to avoid making a concrete statement. Washington, however, has been clear in advocating that the stipulations of international organizations and internationally accepted rules should be followed in resolving such issues. The USA has also been unequivocal in its support for South Korea's desire to conduct military exercises within ROK territorial waters, including exercises involving aircraft carriers. Beijing has chided Seoul for conducting certain types of military exercises inside the ROK's territorial waters, especially joint exercises with the USA, and has sought to curtail and regulate the South Korean navy's activities (Harold, 2012: 299; 304; Kim Young-jin, 18/09/2012).

The Yellow Sea's geographical location in close proximity to some of the PRC's key urban centers and military installations means that Beijing is very sensitive about such joint exercises (Yoon, 2015: 1). At the same time, however, it is noted that Kang has claimed if China is too adamant in its call for the USA and the ROK to end their joint drills, then China would be placed under greater pressure not to conduct military exercises of its own inside South Korea's EEZ, which has been a point of contention. For this reason, Beijing has opted for a status quo policy and strategic ambiguity in the waters around Socotra Rock (Kim Young-jin, 18/09/2012). This, however, is a potentially precarious balancing act. Since Seoul stepped up its presence and developments on Socotra Rock after 2000, the Chinese have tended to react to these activities physically as well as diplomatically. For example, PRC government agency vessels patrolled near the submerged rock in 2003 after the South Koreans had completed the Ieodo Ocean Research Station ("China sent gov't vessel", 27/07/2011). While the Sea of Japan and the Yellow Sea have been carefully defended to ward off any possible threat from Japan over the Liancourt Rocks, and a sometimes violent North Korea over maritime borders and the islands of Yeonpyeong and Baengnyeong, Koh lamented in 2011 that until recently the Seoul government 'paid relatively scant attention' to the East China Sea. This sea, he claims, is South Korea's most vital maritime lifeline because virtually all of the country's exports and imports pass through it. Due to the fact that no bilaterally agreed median line exists between the two countries which could delineate EEZ and continental shelf rights, Koh has called on the Seoul government to do everything it can to face down 'potential Chinese provocation around Ieodo' (Koh, 16/11/2011).

South Korean concerns about its maritime security were also expressed in 2005 when the ROK's Ministry of National Defense publicized the details of a 15-year military modernization program, Defense Reform 2020 (DR 2020). The main objective the program envisaged was the development of a modern blue water navy, the transformation to be characterized by a reduction in manpower to an increase in technology, and a move from being military-dominated to civilian-dominated. However, due to a change of administrations and Defense Ministers in the years immediately following, as well as North Korea's March 2010 torpedo attack on the ROK navy corvette *Cheonan*, DR 2020 was never implemented. Instead, it was replaced by Defense Reform Plan 307 (DRP 307) in March 2011 (Park Hwee Rhak, 2014: 379).[2]

During his time in office from 13 February 2008, ROK President Lee Myung-bak had expressed his support for the DR 2020 plan and emphasized the need for strengthened maritime capabilities (Roehrig, 2012: 63). South Korea has since been taking more strident measures to address security in and around Socotra Rock. Despite this recognition of the need for reform, analysts note the dilemma for South Korea is due to the fact that it will be impossible for the ROK to balance itself against the PRC'S future military strength and development. At the same time, there are many incentives to keep relations positive with the Chinese (Roehrig, 2012: 76). The South Koreans have also shown some sensitivity to Chinese concerns, for example, with regards to intelligence-sharing proposals with the PRC (Chung Min-uck, 13/07/2012).

China's Security Concerns

For their part, Chinese military planners have grown increasingly sensitive to the security connotations of Seoul's defense changes and upgrades in recent years, where Socotra Rock and the neighboring Jeju Island have taken on a greater military significance. As the PRC has enhanced its capabilities in maritime areas since the late 1980s, it has likewise enhanced its presence in the East China Sea as well as the South China Sea. In December 2011, for example, Beijing dispatched its largest surveillance patrol ship, the 3000-ton *Haijian 50*, on its maiden voyage and sent it to the East China Sea. According to Liu Zhendong, the head of the East China Sea Fleet of China Marine Surveillance, a maritime law enforcement agency, the journey was to entail protecting the country's marine rights and territorial rights in areas such as Rixiang Rock, Suyan Rock, and the Chunxiao and Pinghu gas fields.[3] The domestically constructed ship dwarfs the 1000-ton surveillance ships which the PRC normally uses, and includes a helicopter landing pad, and the country's most advanced marine technology. Moreover, May 2010 had also seen the Chinese authorities release the document *Ocean Development Report*, which warned that the state's rights and interests in maritime areas were in a difficult and complicated position. It also noted that the country needed to protect itself against numerous 'safety threats', which included terrorism and disagreements over maritime resources, sovereignty, and maritime boundaries ("China sends leading patrol ship", 13/12/2011).

There was also a *Global Times* article written only a few weeks later in January 2012, which called for action and not protest to save what were allegedly China's islands from environmental as well as other threats. It went on to declare that these features 'are not only nature's gifts' but 'also important vessels of national sovereignty, oceanic rights and sites of major national interest'. The piece also noted the increasing threats and 'frequent bouts of conflict' since the 1970s, which the country faces with eight of its neighbors over 'China's islands'. This threat, it claims, has seen 'the fracturing of its sea lanes, the invasion of its islands, and the exploitation of its oceanic resources'. Japan's claim to the Diaoyu Islands and 'South Korea's confiscation of Suyan Rock, which it renamed Parangdo' [sic], and Seoul's 'more recent saber-rattling over the Rixiang Reef in the Yellow Sea' are all cited as evidence of this threat to China's security.[4] For these reasons, the article argues that damage already done to the state's sovereign rights 'cannot be easily be undone' and 'when solemn protest fails, what other recourse does it have?' China should therefore 'contemplate all the options for protecting the country's territorial integrity'. In addition, the article refers to the implementation of the March 2010 'Law of the People's Republic of China on Island Protection', which outlines the PRC's legal rights to stewardship in its peripheral waters as well as a possible framework for a peaceful resolution of disputes. However, it also laments that 'unfortunately, with so many actors in this sea drama working outside legal channels, there's only so much the law can do' (Wang Xiaobo, 16/01/2012).

While such articles are arguably written for foreign consumption aimed at emphasizing China's resolve, they do reflect a growing sense of frustration over the speed at which neighbors are strengthening their claims over 'Chinese' maritime territory. They also illustrate how a more powerful PRC with enhanced maritime capabilities has become less willing to sit back silently while rivals buttress their position on features such as Socotra Rock. Until now, Beijing's responses on this issue have been quite measured and controlled. Recent security developments such as the construction of a major naval base on Jeju island in close proximity to the feature, however, will no doubt influence how Chinese decision-makers perceive South Korean activities in relation to the rock.

The website of the Korea Hydrographic and Oceanographic Agency (KHOA) emphasizes the necessity of the IORS not only acting in accordance with international law and defending the ROK's national interests, but also in dealing with natural disasters, investigating climate change, and improving maritime safety (Korea Hydrographic and Oceanographic Agency, 2010). Shim Jae Seol, the Director of the Climate Change and

Coastal Disaster Research Department at the Korea Ocean Research & Development Institute, also defends the station's purpose, noting that 'more than 100,000 ships pass Ieodo' every year. As such, the research station with its lighthouse and helicopter landing pad plays an important role as a rescue facility in responding to numerous maritime accidents which take place in the area (Flenniken, 14/08/2011).

The Jeju Civilian-Military Port

Beijing, however, has not been reassured by such claims nor by Seoul's plans for the nearby, strategically well-placed Jeju Island. In January 2011, the South Korean navy commenced spending US $970 million in construction activities for a new military base. Officially referred to as the Jeju Civilian-Military Complex Port, it is located in Gangjeong, Jeju Island, and is the largest dual civilian-military port in South Korea. According to a Korean naval source cited in the New York Times in August 2011, the new state-of-the-art facility will serve as a base for up to 20 warships as well as submarines. Originally scheduled to be completed in 2014, but in fact officially opened in February 2016 after numerous delays and protests, the aim of the military base is to protect South Korea's vital oil-dependent and export-driven shipping lanes. It will also permit the South Koreans to respond faster to any incident with the PRC over Socotra Rock. The new port has simultaneous mooring capacities for up to 20 warships, three submarines, and two large cruise ships. The facility also permits the ROK to not only respond quicker to any maritime threat from neighboring states, but particularly in regard to North Korea, and to protect vital shipping lanes in any of the three seas that touch upon the Korean Peninsula ("Jeju naval base", 29/02/2016). It has also been mentioned that both countries believe the feature is surrounded by oil and mineral deposits (Choe, 19/08/2011).

Interestingly, one of the port's key objectives is the promotion of cruise tourism from major ports in China. An article in late 2017 reported on the test visit of the massive cruise ship *Quantum of the Seas* from Shanghai to Jeju. With a capacity of 168,666 tons, and carrying 4905 passengers and 1500 staff members, the passengers remained on the ship since the cruise ship terminal was not due to be completed until March 2018 (Kim, D. H., 29/09/2017). If the Terminal High-Altitude Area Defense (THAAD) controversy of 2016 and 2017 and subsequent economic boycotts by Chinese consumers are anything to go by, then the cruise port's fortunes could be dependent on how South Korea and its US allies address bilateral challenges such as missile defense, fisheries, Socotra Rock, and other issues. A warning about this has been raised in a state-sponsored Chinese newspaper and is discussed further on.

The strategic desire to enhance the response time to events in and around Socotra Rock and to demonstrate South Korea's ability to exercise its sovereignty within its EEZ waters was also reflected in the government's November 2011 launch of a high-speed and high-tech survey vessel, which would be used for transportation and research purposes by the marine research station. The presence of this vessel also means that it would now just take three hours to travel from Socotra Rock to Jeju rather than the normal eight hours for regular ships. According to the Ministry of Land, Transport and Maritime Affairs, the 90-ton *Haeyang Nuri* can travel at a maximum speed of 35 knots, and cost ₩8.2 billion (US $7.2 million) to construct ("S. Korea launches boat", 18/11/2011). The ship, which falls under the authority of the Korea Hydrographic and Oceanographic Administration (KHOA), will survey the sea and seabed as well as the safety of essential shipping lanes in the waters between Socotra Rock and Jeju. It will also gather information on the ocean environment, upcoming weather hazards, and forecasts, as well as the effects of pollution (Koh, 16/11/2011). The enhancement of Seoul's position vis-à-vis overlapping EEZs and Socotra Rock, as well as a strengthened naval stance via the Jeju naval base, has no doubt complicated the approaches open to a strategically threatened China in any attempts to resolve these maritime disagreements. Recent media reports of the US navy conducting underwater surveys in waters close to the naval base have made China more anxious about the likelihood of a deployment of US strategic assets at the port. Representatives for the base have tried to play down these reports, stating that such surveys are standard practice at all major ports and are defensive measures aimed at protecting US and ROK vessels against possible submarine and mine attacks ("U.S. naval ship conducted", 04/09/2017).

Despite such explanations, the apparent increased militarization of the waters around Socotra Rock and Jeju has caused considerable discomfort not just in China but also in South Korea. Here, left-wing and right-wing activists, environmentalists, and Jeju residents all vie to have their voices, both for and against the base, heard. One reason for the anti-base protests is a prevailing fear, as mentioned above, that US warships will be allowed to dock at the base. There has also been a strong suspicion that the key purpose of the base is not to defend the ROK or Japan against North Korean missiles, but rather to serve as an outpost from which the USA can project its power against the PRC right on its own doorstep (Choe, 19/08/2011). The Korean right-wing media, however, support the move as one which will enhance the country's security because it will act as a deterrent against potential Chinese aggression. The presence of missile batteries on Jeju would also allow for a rapid firing of missiles in the event of a serious confrontation over Ieodo (Choe, 19/08/2011).

Korean anti-base activists such as Choi Sung-hui, however, appreciate what the base issue would mean for Jeju and perhaps Socotra Rock when he commented, 'in case of tension between the United States and China, Jeju … the military pressure point closest to China … would be one of the first objectives' ("In South Korea, a tiny fishing village", 13/10/2011). Another Korean anti-base activist warned that if the Americans ever use Jeju as a means to threaten the strangulation of the PRC, then the Chinese will react at first with diplomatic methods such as economic retaliation and travel restrictions. If frictions, however, rose beyond this to a dangerous level, then Beijing could order a maritime blockade or even a retaliatory attack. Conservative sources in the ROK have been deeply critical of these anti-base protesters. On 13 March 2012, for example, the conservative Chosun Ilbo newspaper ran an editorial entitled 'Naval Base Protesters are Dangerously Naïve', which emphasized the importance of the base for defending Socotra Rock and the threat posed by PRC's first aircraft carrier, the *Liaoning* in adjacent waters in the future. The aircraft carrier subsequently entered service in September 2012. The editorial also mocked those who were opposed to these defensive measures in regard to Jeju and similar cases, commenting 'maybe the protesters would like to gift-wrap the rocks when that happens and hand them over to China' ("Naval base protestors are", 13/03/2012; "China's first aircraft carrier", 25/09/2012).

Seoul has tried to expand its naval capabilities while balancing requests from Washington and Beijing. One of its most controversial moves was to proceed with the construction of KDX-III destroyers, which have been fitted with the US-designed Aegis Ballistic Missile Defense (ABMD) missile-intercepting system. The presence of state-of-the-art destroyers equipped with the ABMD system at Jeju will also strengthen the USA and South Korea's relative position vis-à-vis the PRC. These will provide South Korea and Japan with a protective shield against both Chinese and North Korean missiles, even though the extent to which they could prevent a

DPRK missile strike on the south is questionable. Beijing made serious protests about this development in 2004 (Choe, 19/08/2011). This took place in addition to the flare-up over the THAAD issue in 2016 and 2017, mentioned earlier in this chapter and discussed in Chap. 3.

From China's perspective, its concerns about Jeju and its environs are not unfounded. In March 2011, the US Under-Secretary of State for Arms Control and International Security, Ellen O. Tauscher, stated that Washington was trying to persuade Seoul to enhance their bilateral missile defense ties, a move which some experts viewed as one focused on the rising China. Nevertheless, one scholar, John F. Fei of the RAND Corporation, noted in 2011 how the Jeju base project might reflect a change in South Korean attitudes toward the rising PRC, which had predominantly tended to see their giant neighbor as an economic threat. By 2011, however, Seoul 'no longer repressed voices within the elite calling for a more muscular political and security posture to hedge against China' (Choe, 19/08/2011). In this context, the issue of Socotra Rock, EEZ and continental shelf claims, and the related exercise of authority in adjacent waters should be not viewed as a merely legal disagreement but also as an issue interlinked with some serious defense concerns on both sides. Chinese concerns are reflected in PRC media publications such as the *Global Times*, where strongly worded articles have been used to convey veiled threats expressing Chinese anger with South Korea's defense shifts on their maritime periphery. In an article titled 'South Korea turns tourist resort into weapon', the newspaper lamented the building of a naval base which US troops would use 'as a strategic outpost to contain China and ensure the regional ocean hegemony of the US' (Chao Lv, 07/09/2011).

The same article also notes how the base will be used to counter the threat of Chinese inter-continental ballistic missiles and 'may also be used' in a conflict over Socotra Rock, reflecting South Korea's 'thorough fear' of China and the imprudent willingness of Seoul to risk peace in the region for its own military objectives. As a result, what was once a tourist island of world peace, after official designation in 2005, will soon become a 'weapon aimed at its neighbor'. In response to this action by Seoul, whom the writer claimed 'wants to earn the money of Chinese tourists and threaten the tourists' home country by force at the same time', the article's author proposed an idea. He suggests that the 300,000 or so Chinese tourists and business people who visit Jeju every year and spend hundreds of billions of Korean won should boycott the island and let it 'disappear on the map of China's huge tourism market' (Chao Lv, 07/09/2011).

China also reacted angrily to an announcement from Seoul in 2012 regarding South Korea's new naval fleet plans for the sensitive Socotra Rock and the Liancourt Rock features. The Korean Donga.com website cites a commentator with the Chinese Shenzhen Satellite TV company, in a broadcast carried by other networks, for example, who complained that the fleet's launch was all part of a new and worrying Washington-inspired defense strategy which would allow the USA to fight two wars at once. The defense moves were also aimed at permitting South Korea to enhance its own independent reconnaissance and attack capabilities and reflected Seoul's 'military ambition' ("Chinese media react sensitively", 10/01/2012). At the time of this writing it is apparent that more complex and yet vital security considerations have been incorporated into the question of whose jurisdiction extends over the waters of Socotra Rock.

Notes

1. See Mario Esteban, 'The Management of Nationalism During the Jiang Era (1994–2002) and Its Implications on Government and Regime Legitimacy', *European Journal of East Asian Studies* 5, no. 2 (2006): 181–214.
2. Chun In-Bum (31/10/2017), 'Korean defense reform: History and challenges': https://www.brookings.edu/research/korean-defense-reform-history-and-challenges/.
3. Rixiang Rock is *Gageocho* in Korean, and also known as *Gageo Reef*; Chunxiao and Pinghu are known in Japanese as *Shirakaba* and *Kikyo*, respectively.
4. This reference to Suyan Rock being renamed as *Parangdo* is not correct. In fact, *Parangdo* has been used in the mythology of the feature, as has *Ieodo*. However, in 2001 *Ieodo* was formally selected as the official name.

Bibliography

Albert, Eleanor. "The China – North Korea Relationship." *Council on Foreign Relations* (CFR), 28/03/2018. https://www.cfr.org/backgrounder/china-north-korea-relationship

Cai, Jian. "ADIZ dispute not decisive factor in Sino-Korean ties." *Global Times*, 18/12/2013. http://www.globaltimes.cn/content/832873.shtml

Chao, Lv. "South Korea turns tourist resort into weapon." *Global Times*, 07/09/2011. http://english.people.com.cn/90780/7590463.html

China Expresses 'Grave Concern, Opposition' to N. Korea Missile Test (29/11/2017), *KBS World Radio*. http://world.kbs.co.kr/english/news/news_In_detail.htm?No=132043

China sends leading patrol ship to East China Sea on maiden voyage (13/12/2011), *Xinhua*. http://news.xinhuanet.com/english/china/2011-12/13/c_131304219.html

China sent gov't vessel to claim Korea's Ieo Island (27/07/2011), *Dong-A Ilbo*. http://english.donga.com/srv/service.php3?biid=2011072774718

China's first aircraft carrier enters service (25/09/2012), *BBC News*. http://www.bbc.com/news/world-asia-china-19710040

Chinese media react sensitively to Korea's naval fleet plans (10/01/2012), *Dong-a Ilbo*. http://english.donga.com/srv/service.php3?biid=2012011014478

Choe, Sang-Hun. "Island's Naval Base Stirs Opposition in South Korea." *New York Times*, 19/08/2011. http://www.nytimes.com/2011/08/19/world/asia/19base.html?pagewanted=all

Chung, Min-uck. "Seoul proposes military pact with Beijing." *Korea Times*, 13/07/2012. http://www.koreatimes.co.kr/www/news/nation/2012/07/116_115054.html

Flenniken, Lauren. "Claiming Ieodo Rock: Maritime boundary disputes remain deadlocked between South Korea and China." *Jeju Weekly*, 14/08/2011. http://www.jejuweekly.com/news/articleView.html?idxno=1829

Harold, Scott W. "Ieodo as Metaphor? The Growing Importance of Sovereignty Disputes in South Korea–China Relations and the Role of the United States," *Asian Perspective* 36, no. 2 (April–June 2012): 287–307.

In South Korea, A Tiny Fishing Village Engulfed In A Geopolitical Maelstrom (13/10/2011), *World Crunch*. http://www.worldcrunch.com/south-korea-tiny-fishing-village-engulfed-geopolitical-maelstrom/3931

Jeju naval base (29/02/2016), *Korea Herald*. http://www.koreaherald.com/view.php?ud=20160229001123

Kim, D.H. "A Cruise Ship Arrived at Jeju Civilian – Military Complex Port for the First Time." *The Jeju Weekly*, 29/09/2017. http://www.jejuweekly.com/news/articleView.html?idxno=5696

Kim, Ga Young. "WPK lays out scathing new approach in relations with China." Daily NK, 31/03/2016. http://english.dailynk.com/english/read.php?cataId=nk00100&num=13836

Kim, Young-jin. "Why Ieodo matters." *Korea Times*, 18/09/2012. http://www.koreatimes.co.kr/www/news/nation/2012/09/117_120266.html

Koh, Choong-suk. "New boat plying from Jeju to Ieodo." *Korea Times*, 16/11/2011. http://www.koreatimes.co.kr/www/news/opinon/2012/02/198_98884.html

Korea Customs Service. "Import/Export by Country." 2018. http://www.customs.go.kr/kcshome/trade/TradeCountryList.do

Korea Hydrographic and Oceanographic Agency. "Ieodo." 2010. http://eng.khoa.go.kr/kcom/cnt/selectContentsPage.do?cntId=ieodo_submain

Lind, Jennifer. "Will Trump's hardball tactics work on China and North Korea?" *CNN*, 07/08/2017. https://edition.cnn.com/2017/08/07/opinions/china-north-korea-opinion-lind/index.html

Naval Base Protesters Are Dangerously Naïve (13/03/2012), *Chosun Ilbo*. http://english.chosun.com/site/data/html_dir/2012/03/13/2012031301525.html

Park, Hwee Rhak. "South Korea's Failure to Implement 'Defense Reform 2020'." *Korean Journal of International Studies* 12, no. 2 (December 2014): 379–401.

Roehrig, Terence. "Republic of Korea Navy and China's Rise: Balancing Competing Priorities." In *CNA Maritime Asia Project Workshop Two: Naval Developments in Asia*, edited by Michael A. McDevitt and Catherine K. Lea, 61–78. Alexandria, Va.: Center for Naval Analyses, 2012.

S. Korea launches boat to service Ieodo research station (18/11/2011), *Yonhap News Agency*. http://english.yonhapnews.co.kr/news/2011/11/18/0200000000AEN20111118002100320.html

U.S. naval ship conducted undersea survey off Jeju base: local official (04/09/2017), *Yonhap News Agency*. http://english.yonhapnews.co.kr/news/2017/09/04/38/0200000000AEN20170904012600315F.html

Van Dyke, Jon M. "Ieodo." *Maritime Boundary Disputes in the East China Sea* (conference), Seoul, South Korea, 30/06/2011–01/07/2011.

Wang, Manna. "South Korea and China Conflict Over Islet in East China Sea." *Epoch Times*, 26/08/2007. https://www.theepochtimes.com/south-korea-and-china-conflict-over-islet-in-east-china-sea_1732773.html

Wang, Xiaobo. "Action, not protest, can save China's islands." *Global Times*, 16/01/2012. http://www.globaltimes.cn/content/692369.shtml

Yoon, Sukjoon. "Korea-China Maritime Boundary Talks: Implications for South China Sea." *RSIS Commentary* No. 89, 13 April 2015. https://www.rsis.edu.sg/wp-content/uploads/2015/04/CO15089.pdf

Yun, Yeongmi and Kicheol Park. "Structural Restrictions of Territorial Disputes In Northeast Asia," *Journal of East Asian Affairs* 27, no. 2 (Fall/Winter 2013): 89–117.

CHAPTER 7

Present and Future Considerations

Abstract This chapter discusses present and future considerations surrounding the management and possible resolution of this dispute. It evaluates the possibility of a settlement, and the options open to the two parties, contending that shared or joint-use zones in such areas as fisheries and seabed resources, for example, may serve to reduce frictions while benefitting all the parties concerned. The case is also argued for South Korea revising its contradictory natural prolongation and continental shelf-based claim vis-à-vis Japan elsewhere in the East China Sea. In addition, technological advances in resource extraction, for example, will represent opportunities and challenges for friendlier ties in the future. The chapter asserts that present and future difficulties do not necessarily mean the two neighbors are on an inevitable path to confrontation over this submerged rock.

Keywords East China Sea • Joint-use zones • THAAD controversy

In very recent years and until the spring of 2018, the waters close to and around Socotra Rock have been characterized by a strategic environment that has become increasingly precarious but not yet unmanageable. As elaborated below, there were two particular developments which contributed to this, the first being the fallout from China's November 2013 ADIZ declaration.[1] The second factor was the THAAD controversy of

S. Fox, *China, South Korea, and the Socotra Rock Dispute*,
https://doi.org/10.1007/978-981-13-2077-4_7

2016 and 2017, which only further complicated the stated bilateral desire to repair ties and to engage in confidence-building measures.[2]

Fortunately, while political and economic relations have ostensibly improved following the indefinite thaw in relations in late 2017,[3] observers tend to agree that recent PRC military maneuvers and activities in the northern East China Sea reflect at least two realities, both of which may impact upon approaches to dispute resolution. First, despite the apparent signs of détente, the Chinese are very displeased with the US-ROK alliance and claimed strategic losses over THAAD, the new Jeju naval base, and the airspace over 'Suyan' Rock. The second reality is that China is increasingly eager to demonstrate it has arrived as a serious and capable player on the high seas. In December 2016, for example, the PRC's only battle-ready aircraft carrier, the *Liaoning*, carried out its first live-fire drill, which included missile launches, in the Bohai Sea. Footage of the maneuvers, involving dozens of vessels and aircraft such as destroyers and carrier-launched Shenyang *Flying Shark* J-15 jet fighters, was broadcast on the state-run China Central Television (CCTV) channel. The Chinese are also using the skills developed during the refurbishment of the *Liaoning* (originally purchased from Ukraine) to construct their first domestically produced carrier, an even larger Type 001A vessel (Law, 16/12/2016). On 25 December 2016, the *Liaoning* passed between the Japanese territories of Okinawa and Miyako Island in the southern East China Sea. The Chinese media celebrated the voyage as representative of the PLAN penetrating the first-island chain, a natural strategic barrier which they view as restricting their military's access to the Pacific Ocean (Huang, 10/01/2017). The question of whether or not China will more assertively back up its claims in sensitive waters with their new capabilities in potential standoffs with South Korea as well as its ally, the USA, represents a major conundrum for present and future defense planners.

In early January 2017 a significant Chinese presence flew into the KADIZ without notifying the ROK authorities in advance. It consisted of at least eight Chinese military planes, which included six nuclear-capable H-6 strategic bombers, which is rare, a Shaanxi Y-8 early-warning aircraft, and a Shaanxi Y-9 intelligence-gathering plane. They then zigzagged in and out of the aerial zone for more than five hours, staying inside the KADIZ at one point for as long as an hour. The ROK Air Force (ROKAF) issued a warning and scrambled ten of their own aircraft in response. A day later, the Joint Chiefs of Staff (JCS) confirmed that the aircraft had first entered the zone in an area close to Socotra Rock, one of the locations at which the air defense zones of China, Japan, and Korea overlap. One JCS official commented afterward that People's Liberation Army Air Force (PLAAF) planes had crossed over into the Korean zone 'dozens of times' in the previous year and that 'they usually enter in the direction of Ieodo'. According to Kim and Lee, the intrusion was viewed by observers as another sign of Beijing's ire over Seoul's plan to deploy the US-led THAAD system, which is claimed to be an infringement of national strategic interests (S. Kim, Sarah & Lee Chul-jae, 11/01/2017). Noting the significance of the aerial incursion, Jang Kwang-il, a professor at the ROK's Dongyang University and a former Deputy Minister for Policy at the Ministry of National Defense observed: 'Seeing the scale of the entry and the time, it does not seem like a simple military drill or reconnaissance activities' and that rather 'It is a warning message from China to Korea and Japan amid discord over the deployment of the THAAD battery and the East China Sea sovereignty dispute'. He also noted the significance of the H-6 bombers, which he described as the Chinese equivalent of the US B-52 Stratofortress strategic bombers: 'Whenever there is a provocation by North Korea, the United States sends its B-52 bombers to the Korean Peninsula' and 'China sending a large number of its H-6s is a sign of armed protest' (Kim, Sarah & Lee Chul-jae, 11/01/2017). Li Jie, a naval expert in Beijing, supports such views, stating, 'It's rare for China to dispatch so many advanced bombers at the same time' and how it, 'signals that China will not only step up its presence in the Western Pacific, but also in the Sea of Japan and other waters it has interests in' (Huang, 10/01/2017).

As noted, 2017 saw an upsurge in tensions, particularly with regards to the DPRK, and as a consequence the Republic of Korea Navy (ROKN) announced plans late last year to establish an operational aviation command and a new task fleet by 2023. A briefing by the country's Marine Corps, which is calling for a greater operational role in areas around Ieodo for example, also claimed: 'There's a need to establish a unified command system for strategic islands in the East Sea, the Yellow Sea and the South Sea' and cited the improved maritime capabilities of neighboring states as a compelling reason for the call ("S. Korean Navy seeks", 2017). In November 2017, the South Korean media reported on the presence of a US nuclear-powered submarine for the first time at Jeju Naval Base, prompting the appearance of protesters demanding its withdrawal. The USS *Mississippi* (SSN-782), a Virginia-class fast attack vessel, is one of the US military's most state-of-the-art submarines. At that time, as many as six foreign naval vessels, starting with the USS *Stethem* in March 2016, an Aegis destroyer, had been moored at the base since it was completed in February 2016 (Heo, 24/11/2017). On 18 December 2017, South Korean fighter jets scrambled to the KADIZ to escort a number of PRC aircraft out of the zone. These aircraft consisted of two H-6 bombers, two Shenyang J-11 fighter jets, and one TU-154 reconnaissance plane. The Chinese planes entered the zone in the sky above Socotra Rock and had been inside the area for three and a half hours. Over a hotline, they described the activities as a routine exercise (Lotto Persio, 18/12/2017).

Later that month, at a port just south of Incheon, South Korean custom officials, for the second time in a matter of weeks, seized a vessel, the *Koti*. The ship was flying under a Panamanian flag, which they suspected of supplying oil to the DPRK, in contravention of UN sanctions enacted in November 2017. The ship's crew consisted of mostly Chinese and Myanmar nationals. The first seized ship was a Hong Kong-flagged vessel. Such vessels were suspected of transferring oil at sea to DPRK ships. Both China and Russia have been accused of complicity in such activities, and China in particular has been pointed out as obstructing efforts by the USA to blacklist a number of ships suspected of such actions; this is in spite of approving sanctions against North Korea at the United Nations Security Council (UNSC). In response, the Chinese government publicly stated that they always fully and strictly implement Security Council resolutions so long as the measures 'have a basis in conclusive and actual proof' (Park and Jin, 31/12/2017). On 29 January 2018, the JCS reported that a number of air force planes, including a F-15 K fighter, were dispatched to the KADIZ to 'closely monitor' an unannounced intrusion by a Shaanxi Y-9, an unarmed transport plane, which had entered the zone just to the southwest of the submerged rock. The plane proceeded to enter Japan's ADIZ afterward. In total, the plane flew for about four and a half hours before it re-entered Chinese airspace (Doi & Takeda, 30/01/2018).

These incursions have not been confined to the Yellow Sea and northern East China Sea. In late February, a PLAAF fighter jet flew without prior notification inside the KADIZ a mere 55.5 km northwest of Ulleungdo Island off the ROK's east coast and stayed there for more than four hours. The ROKAF dispatched more than ten aircraft in response and, via the South Korea-China military hotline, reportedly warned the Chinese pilot directly to 'stop the act of raising tensions that can trigger an accidental conflict'. According to the JCS, the jetfighter's flight path was 'unusual' and the incident represented the closest any unauthorized

Chinese military aircraft had ever come to South Korea's eastern coast. This worrying development occurred in the midst of an apparent détente following a serious downturn in bilateral ties over the THAAD controversy (Panda, 28/02/2018).

Understandably there is bound to be concern from the perspective of South Korea despite various verbal assurances and statements by the PRC. Despite an unprecedented upturn in inter-Korean relations that year, such actions no doubt cause apprehensions when trying to decipher the true nature and aims of Beijing's activities inside their country's own designated maritime and aerial zones.[4] The future at best seems to offer only more of the same, though an overall review might prompt some additional perspectives.

Reviewing the Context

We need to remember that prior to the 1990s, it is apparent that Socotra Rock was an occasional but very minor irritant in bilateral ties between South Korea and China. However, following Seoul's construction of a research station in 2003 and Beijing's reactions to it, the issue was placed on a higher plain within the wider relationship and came to play a more prominent role in recent bilateral relations. This has coincided with Beijing's more assertive verbal and physical defense of its maritime claims since the 1990s as well as growing Chinese fears over the recent construction of the nearby Jeju Island naval base.

The developments and their implications that have brought the dispute to the present forefront of Sino-South Korean relations are now ripe to begin a new stage of more comprehensive exploration and discussion, something this work has aimed to initiate. By shifting the focus away from the purely technical and strategic aspects of this dispute, this discussion also revealed a potentially destabilizing correlation between progress on resolving or at least managing the issue and the health and direction of bilateral ties at a given time.

In providing this overview of the Socotra Rock issue, priority was given to a focus on historical background, the limits of international law, bilateral challenges and other factors that complicate approaches to the dispute, and shared commonalities with other maritime disputes. Often the influence of the past as well as the broader contemporary context can tend to be overlooked and thus contribute to further misunderstanding. First, however, it was important to begin with grasping the basics of the issue's fundamental topography and other related details.

Topography and geographical context figure fundamentally into this issue, so describing these before proceeding to other issues, such as the disputed dividing line, Exclusive Economic Zones (EEZs), and continental shelf claims, and South Korea's contentious construction of a research station in 2003 was essential. The important role of Korean legend and folklore was also brought up, reflecting a deep-seated attachment to the rock and underscoring the feature's emotional and cultural value to the Korean people. A historical overview, which included contrasting historical claims, reflected both sides' cultural, historical, navigational, and resource-related ties to the rock. How minor disputes and contradictory positions since then have hindered the full potential for Chinese-Korean cooperation was also covered.

From there it was crucial to explain the central component to the contrasting legal stances adopted by China and South Korea with regards to EEZs and continental shelf rights. Because maritime law is often referred to by both parties, then certain basics of maritime law needed to be understood when examining this topic. Competing claims include China's natural prolongation of the continental shelf and South Korea's more internationally accepted median line solution with the submerged feature located well within Seoul's EEZ. These claims overlap, and as shown, Socotra Rock rests within the overlapping area. It was demonstrated that the crux of the dispute is thus not territorial, but rather one concerning the right to exercise jurisdictional authority while also protecting against 'foreign' intervention. Just where international legal practice tends to stand on these questions of equidistance, proportionality, natural prolongation, jurisdiction, and freedom of navigation was also presented. In addition, it was shown how both states are in breach of the letter and spirit of maritime law, and the reasons why the two sides are unlikely to seek recourse in international arbitration was also covered.

Thus, against the background of topography, history, and law, the influence of wider bilateral and regional challenges could be examined. Here, it particularly noted that there were increasingly fraught ties between the two neighbors since the early 2000s, when the optimism of the 1990s was replaced by more 'realism and mixed feelings'. The rise in bilateral frictions over the feature has come in the midst of wider mutual anxieties about the strategic and economic objectives of the other side. China's concerns are mainly security-based in relation to national defense and access to resources.

Heightened ROK unease regarding rightful jurisdiction over the feature occurred in a context of growing Chinese influence on the peninsula, where South Koreans increasingly felt that a rising China was a threat not only to Korean sovereignty both north and south, but also to its symbols, touching upon sensitivities concerning national identity and dignity. The dispute is also positioned inside the zero-sum game, avoidance-balancing act that exists between the ROK's 'value-based strategic alliance' with allies, the USA and Japan, and its 'strategic co-operative partnership' with China.[5] The tendency of Socotra Rock-related frictions to develop in conjunction with maritime tensions elsewhere involving China—such as in the East China Sea vis-à-vis Japan as well as the South China Sea and five other states—was also important to specify.

Attention was also given to pertinent controversies and agreements directly related to Socotra Rock since the late 1980s and were discussed in detail. China has repeatedly protested South Korean activities in the area, but it was not until the mid-1990s, when the two neighbors ratified the United Nations Convention on the Law of the Sea (UNCLOS) and set their EEZ and continental shelf claims in stone, that the dispute slowly shifted into the bilateral challenge of today. Alongside mutual reassurances, China issued protests against any unilateral activities in the overlapping area, stating they could not take any legal effect. Its more assertive and physical responses to Seoul's activities since 2003 were also described, consisting of contradictory declarations at various PRC governmental levels, and a shift away from purely diplomatic protests. In addition to displays of jurisdictional authority, such as protesting an ROK salvage operation near the feature in 2011, the Chinese adopted stronger language in a context where they viewed the relative strength of their jurisdictional claims as weakening. In the subsequent years, particularly from 2006 onward, thus represented a new chapter in Socotra Rock-related ties, which also reflected the new strategic and security environment in which the two neighbors found themselves. There were also a higher number of sometimes fatal clashes between Chinese fishing vessels and the ROK coastguard in related waters.

The significance of China's controversial and somewhat overlooked ADIZ declaration in November 2013 was also reviewed, both in general and then specific to the Socotra Rock dispute. The move incorporated the airspace over the submerged feature and included identification rules that aircraft entering the unilaterally declared zone would have to obey. It appeared to undermine a tacit bilateral understanding as well as frequently cited assurances by Beijing that the Socotra Rock issue was not about sovereignty. The new Chinese ADIZ overlapped with both South Korea and Japan's own respective ADIZs. This spurred South Korea to conduct military activities, some of them including Japan, aimed at publicly rejecting the new ADIZ while also instructing airlines to ignore it. On the domestic front in South Korea, a key consequence was that the declaration caused many people to better comprehend and appreciate the strategic importance of the area in which Socotra Rock is located. Seoul reacted to Beijing's move by expanding the Korean ADIZ a month later. The ROK's balancing act between sovereignty protection and maintaining stability with the PRC was made more difficult by the 2013 ADIZ development.

The inter-relationship between the Socotra Rock issue and security, domestic political, and economic factors also needed to be placed under scrutiny, including how they have tested and continue to test bilateral ties today and in recent years. China's economic footprint in the ROK has alarmed many South Koreans, who fear that their neighbor has a 'superpower mentality' toward the Korean Peninsula. China's economic and political influence upon North Korea in particular has also raised serious questions. Such issues are intertwined with South Korean popular and elite perceptions of a growing threat. Similarly, it showed how the potentialities of resources near the feature could spur Seoul or Beijing to act more assertively to access them or deny them to the other side. Core security issues were important to bring up, including the maintenance of transportation and supply lifelines, as well as the potential of a greater US security presence in the region and how this impacts the two neighbors' respective views. Both Socotra Rock and Jeju Island have taken on a greater military significance, due in no small part to the construction of the massive Jeju Island naval base. These realities complicate the approaches open to a strategically threatened China in any attempts to resolve this disagreement. A way forward will require some well-grounded reflection as well as carefully applied strategies.

Future Direction

Present and future considerations for the management and possible resolution of this dispute might be evasive but are not unattainable. In evaluating the possibility of a settlement or perhaps a series of settlements, it must be remembered that the Socotra Rock dispute exists at the bilateral and international levels, and as such is bound to be politically complex and sectorally multifaceted, with economic, trade, military, and social factors often at odds with each other. Progress can only proceed slowly, building on the identification of lessons learned and common factors that might be useful for future policy prescription and analysis.

Neither distant nor recent difficulties have to mean that the two neighbors are on an inevitable path to confrontation over this submerged rock; some progress has been made, provocative actions de-escalated, and scenarios as serious as those seen elsewhere in the region have been avoided. When one puts aside the negative aspects of this dispute, it is clear that these are significantly outweighed by more valuable strategic and economic interests for the wider relationship and for the region. However, burgeoning bilateral economic ties have not been accompanied by a more harmonious security relationship. Rather than an overlapping of bilateral security and economic interests over the feature, what can be seen is a clear separation of wider economic interests with security concerns in peripheral waters. In the absence of a formal agreement, the rock issue, when examined on its own, suggests that the realist tenets of maximizing one's own interests and balancing one's power against a potential adversary in an anarchic world continues to be the primary influence among decision-makers in the two countries.

A key question for the future of this dispute is whether or not the two countries can sustain their successful management of problems when incidents arise. Palpable tensions persist in regard to several issues: the Jeju naval base and its relationship to Socotra Rock; contested EEZs; the consequences of the PRC's November 2013 ADIZ declaration; the possibility of an increased US naval presence in the region; the emotive issue of China's rise and EEZ intrusions within South Korea's waters; uncertainties over the PRC's words and actions in maritime areas; and comprehending the complex dynamics of Chinese decision-making. These tensions all will continue to place a significant strain on peaceful approaches to the issue. This is all the more serious in a context where China and South Korea are strengthening their naval capabilities and the means with which to physically enforce their respective claims. As such, the seemingly unimportant Socotra Rock becomes an issue to watch, though some have been less optimistic about the future than others.

One cogent example can be found in an article referencing a 2012 paper jointly authored by scholar Choi Yearn-hong and Koh Choong-suk, president of the Society of Ieodo Research (SIR) based on Jeju Island. They commented, 'Seeking mutual benefits or joint exploration of sea-bed resources is considered wishful thinking, too idealistic and utopian'. Koh and Choi also contended that 'The future will be dictated by changing science and technology. Rocks which have been worthless may be worthwhile in the future by advanced science and technology, and that they may cause more disputes.' As a solution to the question of ownership of such features as Socotra Rock, the authors suggest ownership should rest with the state having the nearest inhabited territory (Kim Young-jin, 18/09/2012). While it is not surprising that two South Korean scholars from the Society of Ieodo Research would advocate the latter, the former view on changing technology making seabed resources more accessible has proven prescient.[6] One need only look at the more intense activity in recent years to stake claims and extract resources amid heightened competition between rival states in once inaccessible parts of Antarctica, the Arctic Circle, and areas closer to home.[7] Whether or not the relevant parties with contrasting claims in the East China Sea can share the resources *and* unilaterally but peacefully extract them, or refrain in perpetuity from doing so, remains a pressing question for the world's fastest growing region. At the same time, technological advances in resource extraction might also represent embryonic opportunities and challenges for cooperation and friendlier ties in the future.

The relevance of this disagreement when compared to other disputes involving the PRC and/or South Korea, particularly in terms of the much more historically and politically sensitive PRC-Japan dispute, also points to an issue which will probably not be definitively resolved in the near future. It likewise suggests that Beijing will hold firm to its interpretations of international maritime law, despite legal trends and the opinions of respected legal scholars, which, in general, support South Korea's position. To date, the PRC's only successful maritime boundary agreement has been with Vietnam in the Gulf of Tonkin when China made greater concessions on a dividing line because Vietnam's long coastline was factored into the resolution.[8]

As the case of Socotra Rock demonstrates, however, the PRC aims for more rather than less so if Beijing cannot convince Seoul otherwise; the ROK's best interests will arguably continue to rest in sticking to its guns in regards to the current median line. Nonetheless, the ambiguities and shortcomings of UNCLOS, and what some might perceive to be its encouragement of assertion and punishment of acquiescence are bound to cause problems whenever one side acts on its stated claims. This is also the case whenever either country interprets a relative weakening of its position on the underwater feature and overlapping EEZs.

One way to mitigate tensions may be through further step-by-step advances in relation to shared or joint-use zones in such areas as fisheries and seabed resources. This would be in addition to agreements that already exist. These may serve to reduce frictions while benefitting all the parties concerned and act as a framework to later build on. The late maritime dispute expert Jon M. Van Dyke, well respected in his field and citing Japan-South Korea fishing cooperation near the Liancourt Rocks, and China-Japan fishing cooperation in the East China Sea, recognized both the need for and potential of such zones in terms of protecting fish stocks through reduced catches, keeping the marine environment clean, and building trust between states. The case is also argued for South Korea to revise its inconsistent natural prolongation and continental shelf-based claim with Japan and adopt a position that conforms to international legal trends. This would also permit the ROK to register protests, without contradictions, over such issues as the choice of baselines used by China, North Korea, and Japan, seen as questionable when held up to the spirit and principles inherent in UNCLOS Articles 7 and 10, dealing with baselines and bays, respectively. South Korea could likewise use that opportunity to review the strength and fairness of its own baseline claims (Van Dyke, 30/06/2011).

In addition, aforementioned technological advances in resource extraction, for example, also have the potential to represent opportunities and challenges for friendlier ties in the future. While the ROK is likely to stand its ground in refusing to revise the demarcation of the median line, a bilaterally agreed approach to, or resolution of, the demarcation question is still arguably the most realistic way in which the two countries can tackle the issue. Seoul certainly appreciates both the dangers and opportunities inherent in a bilaterally negotiated settlement. Beijing's preference for such an approach is well known, most notably because it places the balance of power indisputably in China's favor, and prevents the Chinese from being weakened in negotiations with a conglomerate of states, a situation it fears in approaches to the multi-party South China Sea disputes. A multilateral approach or one which includes the ICJ or the International Tribunal for the Law of the Sea, however, are clearly not viable options without the consent of Beijing. This is also an extremely unlikely course for the PRC given the probable outcome of any such deliberation over Socotra Rock. If legal and security-related limitations were placed on the scope of discussions, this, though challenging, would not necessarily lead to failure if timed strategically.

The Sino-South Korean relationship is simply too important to both sides for positive ties to be destabilized by such frictions as those that have occasionally arisen. Indeed, both governments have thus far successfully navigated through rough waters and generally prevented the issue from hampering bilateral ties to the level seen with Japan and China over the East China Sea or between Seoul and Tokyo over the Liancourt Rocks. In the case of the PRC, it is apparent that when positive bilateral ties and favorable circumstances exist, compromise and agreement can be found even with states having a history of ties that have been fractious and distrustful. In 2008, for example, the Chinese and the Japanese signed an agreement referred to as the 'China-Japan Principled Consensus on the East China Sea Issue', a largely symbolic yet significant 'principled consensus' on the East China Sea which envisaged joint hydrocarbon development within overlapping EEZs.[9] This accord still remains a roadmap for both countries in spite of the dispute's volatility, as seen following a September 2010 ship-ramming incident[10] and the nationalization of Senkaku Shoto (Diaoyu) Islands controversy of 2012. And mentioned earlier, Beijing also compromised on a median line principle with Vietnam in the Gulf of Tonkin in 2000.

Negotiations on the Socotra Rock issue arguably serve to illustrate the practicalities of the median line approach, but also highlight the need to more clearly specify the parameters of UNCLOS rules and principles. Without a review or a tightening of some of the destabilizing ambiguities found within UNCLOS, states will continue to selectively pick and choose those articles within the law which serve their own interests best, and sometimes with harmful consequences for other states. Beijing and Seoul also appreciate that the acquisition of potential valuable ocean and seabed resources will require compromises that will nonetheless benefit all the parties concerned. Japan should also be consulted with regards to any such agreement, which, if successful, could serve as a model to follow, an example for other states involved in similar maritime disputes, particularly in East Asia.

Any future compromise treaty which relates to Socotra Rock could, in a liberalist vein, positively illustrate how mutual economic interests and benefits can persuade states to be flexible and imaginative in negotiations. When an incident occurs, the two governments would work hard to prevent it from destabilizing the more important economic ties between the PRC and South Korea without standing down on their claims in the area. However, it could be argued that Socotra Rock is a cogent example of the inability of the two sides to resolve the dispute: more than a dozen rounds of negotiations point to the limited influence of their economic interactions and of the heightened distrust between the two states.

There is also much to be said for how domestic politics and circumstances could strongly influence how China's leadership deals with an issue like Socotra Rock. The issue's linkage to China's territorial integrity and maritime resources as well as its security in the face of increasing naval capabilities by Washington's ally, South Korea, provides PRC leaders with apparent reasons to avoid appearing weak if they are seen to compromise. For Seoul, standing firm against Korea's historical master pays political dividends, which future leaders may be tempted to exploit further, though perhaps to the detriment of positive maritime ties. A still elusive agreement on the issue suggests that all these considerations yet remain as salient as ever and only prolongs suspicions that the two parties might have to wait a very long time before agreeing on overlapping EEZs.

Despite the challenges, the less sensitive Socotra Rock negotiations (in terms of history and popular sentiment inside the PRC) arguably provide the Chinese government with a rare opportunity to show its willingness to abide by internationally accepted norms and practices. Such a gesture could moderate the fears of neighboring states and fulfill Beijing's desire to be viewed as a responsible power, particularly with regard China's approach to international law in the South China Sea and in the East China Sea. However, the precedent that such a resolution would set and its knock-on effect on China-related disputes elsewhere in terms of pressuring the PRC to follow suit might compel Beijing to stand firm. One can only hope that the two countries can continue to successfully manage the Socotra Rock dispute, to navigate these unprecedented bilateral waters, and to display in words and actions their deep commitment to the wider relationship and to the peace and stability of Northeast Asia.

Notes

1. For expert commentary and Chinese perspectives on the PRC ADIZ declaration, see Michael Swaine, 'Chinese Views and Commentary on the East China Sea Air Defense Identification Zone (ECS ADIZ)', *China Leadership Monitor*, Hoover Institution, Stanford University. 14/03/2014, no. 43: https://www.hoover.org/research/chinese-views-and-commentary-east-china-sea-air-defense-identification-zone.

2. For a recent example of how the conservative right-wing in South Korea exploits heightened security-related tensions with China, see 'Hong unveils security doctrine to drum up conservative support', *Yonhap News*, 19/04/2017: http://english.yonhapnews.co.kr/news/2017/04/19/0200000000AEN20170419009751315.html.
3. See Kristian McGuire, 'China-South Korea Relations: A Delicate Détente', *The Diplomat* (27/02/2018): https://thediplomat.com/2018/02/china-south-korea-relations-a-delicate-detente/.
4. This is not to downplay China's legitimate concerns over the potential strategic threat posed by the missile defense system. For more on why the PRC has protested the ROK's THAAD system, see, 'What is THAAD anti-missile defence system and why is China against it?', 07/03/2017, *Straits Times*: https://www.straitstimes.com/asia/east-asia/what-is-thaad-anti-missile-defence-system-and-why-is-china-against-it; and Michael D. Swaine, 'Chinese Views on South Korea's Deployment of Terminal High Altitude Area Defense (THAAD)', 14/02/2017, *Chinese Leadership Monitor*, no. 52, Hoover Institution, Stanford University: https://www.hoover.org/research/chinese-views-south-koreas-deployment-thaad.
5. For enhanced relations between the ROK and the PRC, see Peter Murphy, 'The Limits of the Japan–South Korea Military Relationship—Could Japan Lose South Korea to China?', 21/09/2016, *The Diplomat*: https://thediplomat.com/2016/09/the-limits-of-the-japan-south-korea-military-relationship/.
6. For more on a subsequent conference, see Do Je-hae, '"One Ocean Forum" proposed for maritime disputes in East Asia', 28/09/2014, *Korea Times*: http://www.koreatimes.co.kr/www/news/nation/2014/09/359_165367.html.
7. For examples, see Jeremy Bender, 'Russia and China are drastically scaling up their presence in Antarctica', 05/01/2016, *Business Insider*: http://www.businessinsider.com/russia-china-scaling-up-antarctic-presence-2015-12; Basia Rosenbaum, 'The Battle for Arctic Oil', 09/03/2015, *Harvard International Review*: http://hir.harvard.edu/article/?a=10586; Tim Daiss, 'How Oil Drives the South China Sea Conflict', 14/03/2018, *OilPrice.com*: https://oilprice.com/Energy/Energy-General/How-Oil-Drives-The-South-China-Sea-Conflict.html; Viola Zhou, Viola, 'China's deep-sea mission to mine the wealth beneath the ocean floor', 06/10/2016, *South China Morning Post*: http://www.scmp.com/news/china/policies-politics/article/2025456/chinas-deep-sea-mission-mine-wealth-beneath-ocean-floor.
8. For more on this China-Vietnam agreement see Benoit de Tréglodé, 'Maritime Boundary Delimitation and Sino-Vietnamese Cooperation in the Gulf of Tonkin', transl. David Buchanan, *China Perspectives*, 3 (2016):

33–41; Zou Keyuan, 'The Sino-Vietnamese Agreement on Maritime Boundary Delimitation in the Gulf of Tonkin', *Ocean Development & International Law*, 36, no. 1: 13–24.

9. See http://www.mofa.go.jp/files/000091726.pdf.
10. See Wada, 2010.

Bibliography

Doi, Takateru and Hajimu Takeda. "Japan, S. Korea scramble jets to ward off Chinese military planes." *Asahi Shimbun*, 30/01/2018. http://www.asahi.com/ajw/articles/AJ201801300046.html

Heo, Ho-joon. "American nuclear submarine enters Jeju Naval Base." *Hankyoreh*, 24/11/2017. http://www.hani.co.kr/arti/english_edition/e_international/820635.html

Huang, Kristin. "Japan, South Korea scramble fighter jets after eight Chinese warplanes fly over Korea Strait." *South China Morning Post*, 10/01/2017. http://www.scmp.com/news/china/diplomacy-defence/article/2060823/japan-and-south-korea-scramble-fighter-jets-8-chinese

Kim, Sarah and Lee Chul-jae. "Chinese planes penetrate Korea's ADIZ." *Korea JoongAng Daily*, 11/01/2017. http://koreajoongangdaily.joins.com/news/article/article.aspx?aid=3028512

Kim, Young-jin. "Why Ieodo matters." *Korea Times*, 18/09/2012. http://www.koreatimes.co.kr/www/news/nation/2012/09/117_120266.html

Law, Violet. "China's Liaoning aircraft carrier conducts first live-fire drill as Beijing shows off military might." *South China Morning Post*, 16/12/2016. http://www.scmp.com/news/china/diplomacy-defence/article/2055138/chinas-liaoning-aircraft-carrier-conducts-first-live

Lotto, Sofia Persio. "Chinese Warplanes Enter Korea Air Defense Zone, Prompting South Korea to Scramble Fighter Jets," *Newsweek*, 18/12/2017. http://www.newsweek.com/chinese-warplanes-enter-korea-air-defense-zone-south-korea-scramble-fighter-750918

Panda, Ankit. "Chinese Fighter Violates South Korea's Air Defense Identification Zone." *The Diplomat*, 28/02/2018. https://thediplomat.com/2018/02/chinese-fighter-violates-south-koreas-air-defense-identification-zone/

Park, Yuna and Hyunjoo Jin. "S.Korea seizes 2nd ship suspected of providing oil to N.Korea." Reuters, 31/12/2017. https://www.reuters.com/article/us-northkorea-missiles-southkorea-ship/south-koreaseizes-second-ship-suspected-of-providing-oil-to-north-korea-idUSKBN1EP04P

S. Korean Navy seeks aviation command, new task fleet (19/10/2017), *Yonhap News*. http://english.yonhapnews.co.kr/northkorea/2017/10/19/98/0401000000AEN20171019004652315F.html

Van Dyke, Jon M. "Ieodo." *Maritime Boundary Disputes in the East China Sea* (conference), Seoul, South Korea, 30/06/2011–01/07/2011.

Wada, Haruki. "Resolving the China-Japan Conflict Over the Senkaku/Diaoyu Islands." *History News Network*, 31/10/2010. http://www.hnn.us/articles/133059.html

Bibliography

Airbus' aerial tankers to extend operation time up to 4 times (2015-07-02) *Arirang News*. http://arirang.co.kr/news/news_view.asp?nseq=181014&sys_lang=Kor

Albert, Eleanor. "The China – North Korea Relationship." *Council on Foreign Relations* (CFR), 28/03/2018. https://www.cfr.org/backgrounder/china-north-korea-relationship

Amer, Ramses and Li Jianwei. "Maritime Delimitation in the Gulf of Tonkin is Too Important to be Ignored." *ChinaUSFocus*, 29/05/2015. http://www.chinausfocus.com/peace-security/maritime-delimitation-in-the-gulf-of-tonkin-is-too-important-to-be-ignored/

An, Yong-hyun and Jeon Hyok-seok. "Medium 'EEZ Negotiations fast' ... Problems that may arise again." Chosun Ilbo, 02/11/2015. http://news.chosun.com/site/data/html_dir/2015/11/02/2015110200210.html

Baek, Hee Youn. "Legend of Ieodo" (14/08/2011), *Jeju Weekly*. http://www.jejuweekly.com/news/articlePrint.html?idxno=1830

Brunet-Jailly, Emmanuel, ed. *Border Disputes: A Global Encyclopedia, Vol. I–III.* Santa Barbara, CA.: ABC-CLIO, 2015.

Cai, Jian. "ADIZ dispute not decisive factor in Sino-Korean ties." *Global Times*, 18/12/2013. http://www.globaltimes.cn/content/832873.shtml

Caron, David D. and Oral Nilufer. *Navigating Straits: Challenges for International Law*. Leiden: Brill, 2014

Case Concerning the Continental Shelf (Libyan Arab Jamahiriya/Malta) – Judgment of 3 June 1985. *International Court of Justice*, 2015. http://www.icj-cij.org/files/case-related/68/6417.pdf

Cha, Victor. "Korea's Mistake on China's ADIZ Controversy." *Center for Strategic and International Studies, Korea Chair Platform*, 2/12/2013. http://csis.

S. Fox, *China, South Korea, and the Socotra Rock Dispute*,
https://doi.org/10.1007/978-981-13-2077-4

org/files/publication/131202_Koreas_Mistake_on_Chinas_ADIZ_Controversy.pdf

Chang, Jae-soon. "Lee: Ieodo will remain under Korea's control", (12/03/2012), *Korea Times.* http://www.koreatimes.co.kr/www/news/nation/2012/03/116_106770.html

Chao, Lü. "Beijing and Seoul gain much more from close relations." *Global Times*, 18/12/2013. http://epaper.globaltimes.cn/2013-12-19/41389.htm

Chao, Lv. "South Korea turns tourist resort into weapon." *Global Times*, 07/09/2011. http://english.people.com.cn/90780/7590463.html

Charney, Jonathan I. "Progress in International Maritime Boundary Delimitation Law," *American Journal of International Law* 88, no. 2 (1994): 227–256.

Charting the Diaoyus' troubled history (12/10/1996), *South China Morning Post.* http://www.scmp.com/article/177627/charting-diaoyus-troubled-history

Chin, Haeng-Nam. "Conflict over the reef's jurisdiction continues to cast a shadow over Korean and Chinese relations." *Jeju Weekly*, 03/02/2014. http://www.jejuweekly.com/news/articleView.html?idxno=3848

Chin, Haeng-Nam. "Ieodo, where legend and reality meet." *Jeju Weekly*, 2014/02/03. http://www.jejuweekly.com/news/articleView.html?idxno=3848

China Chafes at Korean Observatory on Reef Island (14/09/2006), *Chosun Ilbo.* http://english.chosun.com/site/data/html_dir/2006/09/14/2006091461017.html

China demands S. Korea stop hoisting sunken ship near Ieodo (27/07/2011), *Yonhap News Agency.* http://english.yonhapnews.co.kr/national/2011/07/27/19/0301000000AEN20110727006300315F.html

China disputes S. Korea's ownership of Ieo Island (14/09/2006), *Hankyoreh.* http://english.hani.co.kr/arti/english_edition/e_international/157139.html

China Expresses 'Grave Concern, Opposition' to N. Korea Missile Test (29/11/2017), *KBS World Radio.* http://world.kbs.co.kr/english/news/news_In_detail.htm?No=132043

China expresses regret over S. Korea's move (2013/12/10), *Xinhuanet News.* http://news.xinhuanet.com/english/video/2013-12/10/c_132955189.htm

China Lays Claim to 'Arirang' (23/06/2011), *Chosun Ilbo.* http://english.chosun.com/site/data/html_dir/2011/06/23/2011062301297.html

China, ROK sign free trade agreement (02/06/2015), *China FTA Network.* http://fta.mofcom.gov.cn/enarticle/enkorea/enkoreanews/201506/21876_1.html

China says 'no dispute' with S. Korea over Ieodo in new air zone (25/11/2013), *Korea Observer.* http://www.koreaobserver.com/china-says-dispute-s-korea-ieodo-new-air-zone-14194/

China sends leading patrol ship to East China Sea on maiden voyage (13/12/2011), *Xinhua*. http://news.xinhuanet.com/english/china/2011-12/13/c_131304219.html

China seeks South Korean safety guarantees after warning shots fired at ship (09/12/2015), *Reuters*. http://www.reuters.com/article/us-china-southkorea-idUSKBN0TS0TA20151209

China sent gov't vessel to claim Korea's Ieo Island (27/07/2011), *Dong-A Ilbo*. http://english.donga.com/srv/service.php3?biid=2011072774718

China's first aircraft carrier enters service (25/09/2012), *BBC News*. http://www.bbc.com/news/world-asia-china-19710040

Chinese aircraft intrude S. Korea's air defense identification zone (01/02/2016), *Yonhap News Agency*. http://english.yonhapnews.co.kr/national/2016/02/01/0301000000AEN20160201010500315.html

Chinese Envoy Warns THAAD Deployment Would 'Destroy' Ties (24/02/2016), *Chosun Ilbo*. http://english.chosun.com/site/data/html_dir/2016/02/24/2016022401747.html

Chinese media react sensitively to Korea's naval fleet plans (10/01/2012), *Dong-a Ilbo*. http://english.donga.com/srv/service.php3?biid=2012011014478

Cho, Kye-wan. "South Korea sees biggest worldwide growth in exports in first half of 2017." 20/09/2017. http://english.hani.co.kr/arti/english_edition/e_business/811841.html

Choe, Sang-Hun. "Island's Naval Base Stirs Opposition in South Korea." New York Times, 19/08/2011. http://www.nytimes.com/2011/08/19/world/asia/19base.html?pagewanted=all

Choi, Yearn-hong. 'Ieodo.' *Korea Times*, 25/06/2010. http://www.koreatimes.co.kr/www/news/opinon/2011/04/137_68269.html

Choi, Yearn-hong. "Illegal Chinese Fishing in Korean Waters Gets Worse." *Chosun Ilbo*, 12/11/2011. http://english.chosun.com/site/data/html_dir/2011/11/12/2011111200513.html

Choi, Yearn-hong and Koh Choong-suk. "China's Territorial Ambition." *Maritime Security Asia*, 03/08/2011. http://maritimesecurity.asia/free-2/maritime-security-asia/chinas-territorial-ambition/

Chun, Jin-sung. "Our Dispute with China Isn't About Ancient History." *Chosun Ilbo*, 27/02/2007. http://english.chosun.com/site/data/html_dir/2007/02/27/2007022761035.html

Chung, Jae Ho. "China's "Soft" Clash With South Korea: The History War And Beyond," *Asian Survey* 49, no. 3 (May/June 2009): 468–483.

Chung, Min-uck. "Seoul proposes military pact with Beijing." *Korea Times*, 13/07/2012. http://www.koreatimes.co.kr/www/news/nation/2012/07/116_115054.html

Coast guard conducts emergency exercise near Ieodo (06/09/2011), *Yonhap News Agency*. http://english.yonhapnews.co.kr/news/2011/09/06/0200000000AEN20110906008800320.html

Cohen, Jerome A. and Jon M. Van Dyke. "Finding its Sea Legs." South China MorningPost,26/10/2010.https://www.scmp.com/article/728520/finding-its-sea-legs

Cohen, Jerome A. and Jon M. Van Dyke. "Defusing the Bomb in the East China Sea." *US-Asia Law Institute*, New York University School of Law, November 10, 2010. https://usali.org/publications/defusing-the-bomb-in-the-east-china-sea?rq=Jon%20Van%20Dyke

Delury, John. "North Korea Rents Out Its Resources to Stave Off Reform." *New York Times*, 25/10/2011. http://www.nytimes.com/2011/10/26/world/asia/north-korea-rents-out-its-resources-to-stave-off-reform.html

Do, Jae-ha. "'One Ocean Forum' Proposed for Maritime Disputes in East Asia." *Korea Times*, 28/09/2014. http://www.koreatimes.co.kr/www/nation/2017/04/356_165367.html

Doi, Takateru and Hajimu Takeda. "Japan, S. Korea scramble jets to ward off Chinese military planes." *Asahi Shimbun*, 30/01/2018. http://www.asahi.com/ajw/articles/AJ201801300046.html

Don't Take Peaceful Approach for Granted (25/10/2011), *Global Times*. http://www.globaltimes.cn/content/680694.shtml

Drifte, Reinhard. "From 'Sea of Confrontation' to 'Sea of Peace, Cooperation and Friendship'? – Japan Facing China in the East China Sea," *Japan Aktuell – Journal of Current Japanese Affairs* 16 no. 3 (2008): 27–51.

Drifte, Reinhard. "North East Asia: Territorial Disputes and Divided Countries." Seminar Series 2009 at *Daiwa Foundation Japan House*, London, UK. (18/03/2009). http://www.dajf.org.uk/wp-content/uploads/Prof-Driftes-Presentation.pdf

Drifte, Reinhard. "Territorial Conflicts in the East China Sea – From Missed Opportunities to Negotiation Stalemate," *Asia-Pacific Journal* 7, is. 22, no. 3 (25 May 2009): 1–14. http://apjjf.org/-Reinhard-Drifte/3156/article.pdf

Dzurek, Daniel J. "The People's Republic of China Straight Baseline Claim," *International Boundaries Research Unit Boundary and Security Bulletin* (Summer 1996): 77–87.

Eradicate illegal fishing by Chinese boats in Korean EEZ (05/12/2011), *Yonhap News Agency*. http://english.yonhapnews.co.kr/yhedit/2011/12/05/88/5100000000AEN20111205007600315F.html

Esteban, Mario. "The Management of Nationalism During the Jiang Era (1994–2002) and Its Implications on Government and Regime Legitimacy," *European Journal of East Asian Studies* 5, no. 2 (2006): 181–214.

Fisher, Richard Jr. "South China Sea Competition: China Contemplates More Mischief," *International Assessment and Strategy Center*, 28/06/ 2009. http://www.strategycenter.net/research/pubID.209/pub_detail.asp

Flenniken, Lauren. "Claiming Ieodo Rock: Maritime boundary disputes remain deadlocked between South Korea and China." *Jeju Weekly*, 14/08/2011. http://www.jejuweekly.com/news/articleView.html?idxno=1829

Fox, Senan James. "Uncharted Waters in a New Era: An Actor-Centered Constructivist Liberal Approach to the East China Sea Disputes, 2003–2008." PhD diss., University of Saint Andrews (UK), 2011

Gale, Alastair and Min-Jeong Lee. "South Korea Expands Air-Defense Zone: Move Unlikely to Cause Tension as China Has Accepted Plans." *Wall Street Journal*, 08/12/2013. https://www.wsj.com/articles/south-korea-expands-airdefense-zone-1386484430

Gries, Peter Hays. "The Koguryo Controversy, National Identity, and Sino-Korean Relations Today," *East Asia* 22, Winter 2005, Issue 4, (Winter 2005): 3–17. https://doi.org/10.1007/s12140-005-0001-y

Guo, Rongxing. Territorial Disputes and Resource Management: A Global Handbook. Hauppauge, New York: Nova Publishers, 2006.

Han, Jane. "Ocean Research Center Built for Climate Change" (13/10/2009), *Korea Times.* http://www.koreatimes.co.kr/www/news/biz/2009/10/123_53490.html

Harold, Scott W. "Ieodo as Metaphor? The Growing Importance of Sovereignty Disputes in South Korea–China Relations and the Role of the United States," *Asian Perspective* 36, no. 2 (April–June 2012): 287–307.

Harress, Christopher. "Chinese Military Aircraft Breach Korean and Japanese Air Defense Zones Near To Disputed Ieodo Island." *International Business Times*, 02/02/2016.http://www.ibtimes.com/chinese-military-aircraft-breach-korean-japanese-air-defense-zones-near-disputed-2290227

Heo, Ho-joon. "American nuclear submarine enters Jeju Naval Base." *Hankyoreh*, 24/11/2017. http://www.hani.co.kr/arti/english_edition/e_international/820635.html

Hong, Danbee and Chan-Su Yang. "Classification of Passing Vessels Around the Ieodo Ocean Research Station Using Automatic Identification System," *Journal of the Korean Society for Marine Environment and Energy* 17, no. 4 (November 2014): 1–9. https://doi.org/10.7846/JKOSMEE.12014.17.4.1

Hsiung, James C. "Sea Power, Law of the Sea, and a Sino-Japanese East China Sea 'Resource War.'" In *China and Japan at Odds: Deciphering the Perpetual Conflict*, edited by James C. Hsiung, 133–154. New York: Palgrave Macmillan, 2007.

Hsu, Kimberly. "Air Defense Identification Zone Intended to Provide China Greater Flexibility to Enforce East China Sea Claims." *U.S.-China Economic and Security Review Commission Staff Report*, January 14, 2014. http://www.uscc.gov/sites/default/files/Research/China%20ADIZ%20Staff%20Report.pdf

Huang, Kristin. "Japan, South Korea scramble fighter jets after eight Chinese warplanes fly over Korea Strait." *South China Morning Post*, 10/01/2017. http://www.scmp.com/news/china/diplomacy-defence/article/2060823/japan-and-south-korea-scramble-fighter-jets-8-chinese

Ieodo / Suyan Rock / Socotra Rock, *Global Security*.http://www.globalsecurity.org/military/world/war/socotra-rock.htm

In South Korea, A Tiny Fishing Village Engulfed In A Geopolitical Maelstrom (13/10/2011), *World Crunch*. http://www.worldcrunch.com/south-korea-tiny-fishing-village-engulfed-geopolitical-maelstrom/3931

Institute for Advanced Studies on Asia, University of Tokyo. "The World and Japan Database." http://www.ioc.u-tokyo.ac.jp/~worldjpn/documents/indices/JPKR/index-ENG.html

International Conference to be Held on Korean Island of Ieodo (23/06/2011), *Dokdo Times*. http://dokdotimes.blogspot.com/2011/06/international-conference-to-be-held-on.html

International Court of Justice. "North Sea Continental Shelf Cases: Denmark/Federal Judgement of 20 February 1969". http://www.icj-cij.org/files/case-related/5L1/5537.pdf

Jagota, Naval. "Cause and Effect of the ADIZ over East China Sea." India Administrative Service, June 2013. http://iasscore.in/national-issues/cause-and-effect-of-the-adiz-over-east-china-sea

Japan, S. Korea Hold Joint Sea Drill in China Air Zone (12/12/2013), *Agence France-Presse*. http://www.ndtv.com/world-news/japan-south-korea-hold-joint-sea-drill-in-china-air-zone-544304

Jeju naval base (29/02/2016), *Korea Herald*. http://www.koreaherald.com/view.php?ud=20160229001123

Jeong, Yong-Soo and Sarah Kim. "Korean Navy conducts drill close to Ieodo." *Korea JoongAng Daily*, 04/12/2013. http://koreajoongangdaily.joins.com/news/article/article.aspx?aid=2981469

Ji, Guoxing. "Maritime Jurisdiction in The Three China Seas: Options for Equitable Settlement." *Institute on Global Conflict and Cooperation*, Policy Paper 19 (1995). https://escholarship.org/uc/item/7rq2b069

Jun, Ji-hye. "ROK, US Navies to conduct Ieodo defense training today." *Korea Times*, 03/01/2015. http://www.koreatimes.co.kr/www/news/nation/2015/03/116_174348.html

Jung, Sung-ki. "S. Korea to Ask China to Rectify Claim Over Ieodo." *Korea Times*, 08/08/2008. http://www.koreatimes.co.kr/www/news/nation/2011/04/205_29027.html

Kang, Byeong-Cheol. "Ieodo, Okinotorishima and International Politics," *Society of Ieodo Research* (2012).

Kang, Hyun-kyung. "Ieodo protector sparks imagination of Jeju islanders." *Korea Times*, 12/10/2010. http://www.koreatimes.co.kr/www/news/nation/2016/06/113_77786.html

Kang, Hyun-kyung. "Lee says Ieodo not territorial dispute." *Korea Times*, 12/03/2012. http://www.koreatimes.co.kr/www/news/nation/2012/03/116_106794.html

Kang, Hyun-kyung. "KIPA's new book tackles Dokdo, Ieodo sovereignty." *Korea Times*, 11/10/2012. http://www.koreatimes.co.kr/www/news/nation/2012/10/116_122033.html

Kastner, Jens and Wang Jyh-Perng. "Japan takes a shot at China- via Taiwan." *Asia Times*, 10/07/2010. http://www.atimes.com/atimes/China/LG07Ad01.html

Keck, Zachary. "Chinese Fisherman Killed By South Korea's Coast Guard." *The Diplomat*, 10/10/2014. https://thediplomat.com/2014/10/chinese-fisherman-killed-by-south-koreas-coast-guard/

Keck, Zachary. "South Korea Conducts Military Drill in China's ADIZ." *The Diplomat*, 04/12/2013. https://thediplomat.com/2013/12/south-korea-conducts-military-drill-in-chinas-adiz/

Keck, Zachary. "South Korea to Expand Its Air Defense Identification Zone." *The Diplomat*, 02/12/2013. https://thediplomat.com/2013/12/south-korea-to-expand-its-air-defense-identification-zone/

Kim, Deok-hyun. "S. Korea to toughen rules of engagement against N. Korean attack." *Yonhap News*, 24/11/2010. http://english.yonhapnews.co.kr/national/2010/11/24/86/0301000000AEN20101124012200315F.html

Kim, D.H. "A Cruise Ship Arrived at Jeju Civilian – Military Complex Port for the First Time." *The Jeju Weekly*, 29/09/2017. http://www.jejuweekly.com/news/articleView.html?idxno=5696

Kim, Ga Young. "WPK lays out scathing new approach in relations with China." Daily NK, 31/03/2016. http://english.dailynk.com/english/read.php?cataId=nk00100&num=13836

Kim, Ji-hyun. "China informed Seoul of air defense zone." *Korea Herald*, 25/11/2013. http://www.koreaherald.com/view.php?ud=20131125001000

Kim, Sarah. "Chinese jets breach Korea's ADIZ." *Korea JoongAng Daily*, 03/02/2016. http://koreajoongangdaily.joins.com/news/article/Article.aspx?aid=3014734

Kim, Sarah and Lee Chul-jae. "Chinese planes penetrate Korea's ADIZ." *Korea JoongAng Daily*, 11/01/2017. http://koreajoongangdaily.joins.com/news/article/article.aspx?aid=3028512

Kim, Se-jeong. "Ieodo seminar explores Korea's new frontier." *Korea Times*, 30/06/2011. http://www.koreatimes.co.kr/www/news/nation/2012/02/359_89975.html

Kim, Suk Kyoon. "Understanding Maritime Disputes in Northeast Asia: Issues and Nature," *International Journal of Marine and Coastal Law* 23, no. 2 (2008): 213–247.

Kim, Young-jin. "Why Ieodo matters." *Korea Times*, 18/09/2012. http://www.koreatimes.co.kr/www/news/nation/2012/09/117_120266.html

Koh, Choong-suk. "New boat plying from Jeju to Ieodo." *Korea Times*, 16/11/2011. http://www.koreatimes.co.kr/www/news/opinon/2012/02/198_98884.html

Kor, Kian Beng. "China has wider hopes for Seoul talks, say observers." *Straits Times*, 16/12/2015. http://www.straitstimes.com/asia/east-asia/china-has-wider-hopes-for-seoul-talks-say-observers

Kor, Kian Beng. "Seoul, Beijing to hold talks on overlapping EEZs." *Korea Herald*, 14/12/2015. http://nwww.koreaherald.com/view.php?ud=20151214000883

Kor, Kian Beng. "S. Korea, China to hold talks on sea boundary next month." *Korea Herald*, 07/11/2015. http://www.koreaherald.com/view.php?ud=20151107000046

Korea Customs Service. "Import/Export by Country." 2018. http://www.customs.go.kr/kcshome/trade/TradeCountryList.do

Korea Hydrographic and Oceanographic Agency. "Ieodo." 2010. http://eng.khoa.go.kr/kcom/cnt/selectContentsPage.do?cntId=ieodo_submain

Korea's Coast Guard stations 5,000-ton patrol ship south of Jeju (22/06/2016), *Korea Herald*. http://www.koreaherald.com/view.php?ud=20160622000911

Korea Seeks Fresh Negotiations Over Submerged Rocks (13/03/2012), *Chosun Ilbo*. http://english.chosun.com/site/data/html_dir/2012/03/13/2012031300849.html

Kuo, Lily. "Will a Tiny, Submerged Rock Spark a New Crisis in the East China Sea?" *The Atlantic*, 09/12/2013. http://www.theatlantic.com/china/archive/2013/12/will-a-tiny-submerged-rock-spark-a-new-crisis-in-the-east-china-sea/282155/

Kwon, Yong. "Korea and China's Clashing Histories." *The Diplomat*, 11/07/2014. https://thediplomat.com/2014/07/korea-and-chinas-clashing-histories/

Law, Violet. "China's Liaoning aircraft carrier conducts first live-fire drill as Beijing shows off military might." *South China Morning Post*, 16/12/2016. http://www.scmp.com/news/china/diplomacy-defence/article/2055138/chinas-liaoning-aircraft-carrier-conducts-first-live

Lee, Jae-min. "Equitable share of maritime zone." *Korea Herald*, 29/12/2015. http://www.koreaherald.com/view.php?ud=20151229001062

Lee, Sunny. "Should Korea, China Tackle Sensitive Goguryeo Issue?" *Korea Times*, 28/10/2011. http://www.koreatimes.co.kr/www/news/nation/2014/04/116_97528.html

Legault, Leonard and Blair Hankey. (1993) "Method, Oppositeness and Adjacency, and Proportionality in Maritime Boundary Delimitation," 203–242 in Charney, J.I. and Alexander, L.M. (eds.) *International Maritime Boundaries*, Vol. I, Dordrecht: Martinus Nijhoff. (1996).

Lind, Jennifer. "Will Trump's hardball tactics work on China and North Korea?" *CNN*, 07/08/2017. https://edition.cnn.com/2017/08/07/opinions/china-north-korea-opinion-lind/index.html

Lotto, Sofia Persio. "Chinese Warplanes Enter Korea Air Defense Zone, Prompting South Korea to Scramble Fighter Jets," *Newsweek*, 18/12/2017. http://www.newsweek.com/chinese-warplanes-enter-korea-air-defense-zone-south-korea-scramble-fighter-750918

Luova, Outi. "Transnational Linkages and Development Initiatives in Ethnic Korean Yanbian, Northeast China: "Sweet and Sour" Capital Transfers." *Pacific Affairs* 82, no. 3 (Fall, 2009): 427–446.

Military holds course on Jeju naval base (08/03/2012), *Korea Herald*. http://www.koreaherald.com/view.php?ud=20120308001136&ACE_SEARCH=1

Naval Base Protesters Are Dangerously Naïve (13/03/2012), *Chosun Ilbo*. http://english.chosun.com/site/data/html_dir/2012/03/13/2012031301525.html

'North Korean torpedo' sank South's Navy Ship – Report (20/05/2010), *BBC News*. http://www.bbc.com/news/10129703

Page, Jeremy. "China, South Korea in Row Over Submerged Rock." *Wall Street Journal*, 13/03/2012. http://blogs.wsj.com/chinarealtime/2012/03/13/china-south-korea-in-row-over-submerged-rock/

Pan, Junwu. *Toward a New Framework for Peaceful Settlement of China's Territorial and Boundary Disputes*. Leiden: Martinus Nijhoff Publishers, 2009.

Panda, Ankit. "Everything You Wanted to Know About the USS *Lassen*'s FONOP in the South China Sea." *The Diplomat*, 06/01/2016. http://thediplomat.com/2016/01/everything-you-wanted-to-know-about-the-uss-lassens-fonop-in-the-south-china-sea/

Panda, Ankit. "Chinese Fighter Violates South Korea's Air Defense Identification Zone." *The Diplomat*, 28/02/2018. https://thediplomat.com/2018/02/chinese-fighter-violates-south-koreas-air-defense-identification-zone/

Park, Byong-soo and Park Min-hee. "Stormy seas caused by China's claim to Ieo-do reef." *Hankyoreh*, 12/03/2012. http://english.hani.co.kr/arti/english_edition/e_international/523076.html

Park, Byong-su. "South Korea claims larger continental shelf." *Hankyoreh*, 09/01/2013. http://english.hani.co.kr/arti/english_edition/e_international/568898.html

Park, Choon-Ho. "Maritime Claims in the China Seas: Current State Practices," *San Diego Law Review* 18, no. 3 (April 1981): 443–454.

Park, Hwee Rhak. "South Korea's Failure to Implement 'Defense Reform 2020'." *Korean Journal of International Studies* 12, no. 2 (December 2014): 379–401.

Park, Yuna and Hyunjoo Jin. "S.Korea seizes 2nd ship suspected of providing oil to N.Korea." Reuters, 31/12/2017. https://www.reuters.com/article/us-northkorea-missiles-southkorea-ship/south-koreaseizes-second-ship-suspected-of-providing-oil-to-north-korea-idUSKBN1EP04P

Pedrozo, Raul. "The Bull in the China Shop: Raising Tensions in the Asia-Pacific Region," *International Law Studies* 90, no. 66 (2014): 66–100. https://stockton.usnwc.edu/cgi/viewcontent.cgi?article=1049&context=ils

PRC Foreign Ministry. Press Conference, 14/09/2006. http://www.fmprc.gov.cn/eng/xwfw/s2510/t272110.htm

PRC State Oceanic Administration. 2014. http://english.gov.cn/state_council/2014/10/06/content_281474992889983.htm

PRC Foreign Ministry. Press Conference, 06/11/2015. http://www.fmprc.gov.cn/mfa_eng/xwfw_665399/s2510_665401/t1312707.shtml

President Park holds 1st Korea-China summit in Beijing (28/06/2013), *Korea Net*. http://www.korea.net/NewsFocus/Policies/view?articleId=109560

Raj, Rahul. "South Korean coastguard killed by Chinese fisherman." 12/12/2011. http://www.reuters.com/article/2011/12/12/us-korea-china-idUSTRE7BB03Z20111212

Raj, Rahul. "China's claim on Ieodo." *Korea Times*, 19/01/2016. http://www.koreatimes.co.kr/www/news/opinon/2016/01/162_195794.html

Repeated follies (05/11/2015), *Korea Herald*.http://www.koreaherald.com/view.php?ud=20151105001042

Roehrig, Terence. "Republic of Korea Navy and China's Rise: Balancing Competing Priorities." In *CNA Maritime Asia Project Workshop Two: Naval Developments in Asia*, edited by Michael A. McDevitt and Catherine K. Lea, 61–78. Alexandria, Va.: Center for Naval Analyses, 2012.

ROK Ministry of Foreign Affairs. Press Briefing, 15/03/2012.

ROK Ministry of Foreign Affairs. Press Briefing, 05/11/2015.

ROK Ministry of Foreign Affairs. Press Briefing, 05/07/2016.

Rosenberg, David. "China, neighbors progress in fishery agreements."Asia Times Online, 19/08/2005. http://www.atimes.com/atimes/China/GH19Ad02.html

Rusk Documents. 2012. https://commons.wikimedia.org/wiki/Rusk_documents

Ryall, Julian. "Beijing lays claim to South Korean waters." *The Telegraph*, 23/12/2015. http://www.telegraph.co.uk/news/worldnews/asia/china/12065626/Beijing-lays-claim-to-South-Korean-waters.html

S. Korea, China discuss illegal fishing problem (26/11/2015), *Korea Times*. http://www.koreatimes.co.kr/www/news/nation/2016/05/113_191890.html

S. Korea, China hold first talks on EEZs in 7 years (22/12/2015), *Yonhap News Agency*. http://english.yonhapnews.co.kr/national/2015/12/22/0301000000AEN20151222002053315.html

S. Korea-China maritime border should be drawn at halfway point (23/12/2015), *Donga Ilbo*. http://english.donga.com/List/3/all/26/411940/1

S. Korea, China set up coast guards' hotline (17/12/2015), *Yonhap News Agency*. http://english.yonhapnews.co.kr/news/2015/12/17/0200000000AEN20151217007300315.html

S. Korea Disputes China's Claim Over Ieodo Rocks (12/03/2012), *RTT News*. http://www.rttnews.com/1838718/s-korea-disputes-china-s-claim-over-ieodo-rocks.aspx

S. Korea launches boat to service Ieodo research station (18/11/2011), *Yonhap News Agency*. http://english.yonhapnews.co.kr/news/2011/11/18/0200000000AEN20111118002100320.html

S. Korean Navy seeks aviation command, new task fleet (19/10/2017), *Yonhap News*. http://english.yonhapnews.co.kr/northkorea/2017/10/19/98/0401000000AEN20171019004652315F.html

S. Korea set to submit formal claim on East China Sea shelf to U.N (22/10/2012), *Yonhap News Agency*. http://english.yonhapnews.co.kr/national/2012/10/22/7/0301000000AEN20121022003900315F.html

S. Korea still smarting from China's THAAD retribution (14/03/2018), *Yonhap News Agency*. http://english.yonhapnews.co.kr/news/2018/03/14/0200000000AEN20180314002700320.html

S. Korea toughens penalties for EEZ violation (15/05/2012), *Yonhap News Agency*. http://english.yonhapnews.co.kr/national/2012/05/15/34/0302000000AEN20120515001800320F.html

Seoul-Beijing EEZ talks (23/12/2015), *Korea Times*. http://www.koreatimes.co.kr/www/news/opinon/2015/12/202_193883.html

Seoul takes petty advantage but loses big picture (09/12/2013), *Global Times*. http://www.globaltimes.cn/content/831096.shtml

Shi, Chang-Hoon. "South Korea's Inevitable Expansion of its ADIZ." *Asia Maritime Transparency Initiative*, December 2014. http://amti.csis.org/south-koreas-inevitable-expansion-of-its-adiz/

Shin, Hae-in. "China demanded S. Korea stop activities near Ieodo." *Korea Herald*, 27/07/2011. http://www.koreaherald.com/national/Detail.jsp?newsMLId=20110727000696

Shin, Hyon-hee. "Spats mar 20 years of China ties." *Korea Herald*, 08/08/2012. http://www.koreaherald.com/view.php?ud=20120808001121

Shin, Hyon-hee. "Seoul seeks to bolster drone use in air defense zone." *Korea Herald*, 08/06/2015. http://www.koreaherald.com/view.php?ud=20150608000932

Shin, Hyon-hee. "South Korea fires 249 warning shots at Chinese ships suspected of carrying out illegal fishing in its waters." *The Independent*, 20/12/2017. https://www.independent.co.uk/news/world/asia/south-korea-chinese-finish-boats-warning-shots-illegal-fishing-waters-a8119871.html

Shin, Hyon-hee and Song Sang-ho. "Korea, China, Japan in race over continental shelves." *Korea Herald*, 10/07/2012. http://www.koreaherald.com/view.php?ud=20120710001337

Sino-South Korea Fishing Agreement to Take Effect (04/06/2001), *People's Daily*. http://www.china.org.cn/english/10470.htm

Snyder, Scott. "A Turning Point for China–Korea Relations", *Comparative Connections* 6, no. 3 (July–Sept 2004). http://cc.csis.org/2004/10/turning-point-china-korea-relations/

Snyder, Scott. "China-Korea Relations: Teenage Angst: 15th Anniversary of Diplomatic Relations." *Comparative Connections* (October 2007). http://cc.csis.org/2007/10/teenage-angst-15th-anniversary-diplomatic-relations/

Snyder, Scott and See-won Byun. "China-Korea Relations: A Complex China-ROK Partnership." Comparative Connections 17, no. 3 (January 2016): 97–108.

Song, Sang-ho. "Ieodo not part of territorial dispute with China: Lee." *Korea Herald*, 12/03/2012. http://www.koreaherald.com/national/Detail.jsp?newsMLId=20120312001239

Song, Sang-ho. "China's proposal for EEZ talks sparks Ieodo concerns." *Korea Herald*, 02/11/2015. http://www.koreaherald.com/view.php?ud=20151102001231

Song, Sang-ho. "Seoul, Beijing hold EEZ talks Tuesday." *Korea Herald*, 21/12/2015. http://www.koreaherald.com/view.php?ud=20151221001084

Song, Sang-il. "Ieodo, A Growing Legend." Ieodo Journal 2, (2012).

Song, Yann-huei. "Submerged Geographical Features in the East and South China Seas: An Analysis of the Chinese Claims from the Perspective of the Law of the Sea." Ieodo Journal 2 (2012).

South Korea to deploy 5,000-ton vessel to Ieodo (26/01/2016), *Korea Times*. http://www.koreatimes.co.kr/www/news/nation/2016/01/205_196395.html

Storey, Ian. "Beijing's stance critical in resolution." *Korea Times*, 29/06/2011. http://www.koreatimes.co.kr/www/news/nation/2012/02/359_89860.html

Su Yan jiao (13/03/2012), *China.com.cn*. http://www.china.com.cn/guoqing/2012-03/13/content_24882839.htm

Surhone, Lambert M., Mariam T. Tennoe and Susan F. Henssonow, eds. *Socotra Rock – Reef, Territorial Dispute, Exclusive Economic Zone, Marado, Jeju-do*. Beau Bassin, Mauritius: VDM Publishing, 2010.

Tiezzi, Shannon. "Is China Ready to Solve One of Its Maritime Disputes?" *The Diplomat*, 07/11/2015. http://thediplomat.com/2015/11/is-china-ready-to-solve-one-of-its-maritime-disputes/

Tiezzi, Shannon. "It's Official: China, South Korea Sign Free Trade Agreement." *The Diplomat*, 02/06/2015. http://thediplomat.com/2015/06/its-official-china-south-korea-sign-free-trade-agreement/

Tomale, Diana. "Two Chinese Military Planes Entered South Korea Air Zone." *Korea Portal*, 04/02/2016. http://en.koreaportal.com/articles/16147/20160204/two-chinese-military-planes-entered-south-korea-air-zone.htm

Two Chinese military jets intruded into S. Korea's air defense zone (20/02/2016), *Korea Times*. http://www.koreatimes.co.kr/www/news/nation/2016/02/205_197053.html

United Nations Convention on the Law of the Sea, Montego Bay, Jamaica, 16 November 1994, *United Nations Treaty Series*, vol. 1833. http://www.un.org/depts/los/convention_agreements/texts/unclos/unclos_e.pdf

U.S. naval ship conducted undersea survey off Jeju base: local official (04/09/2017), *Yonhap News Agency*. http://english.yonhapnews.co.kr/news/2017/09/04/38/0200000000AEN20170904012600315F.html

Valencia, Mark J. "The East China Sea Dispute: Context, Claims, Issues, and Possible Solutions," *Asian Perspective* 31, no. 1 (2007): 127–167.

Van Dyke, Jon M. "Ieodo." *Maritime Boundary Disputes in the East China Sea* (conference), Yonsei University, Seoul, South Korea, 30/06/2011–01/07/2011.

Van Dyke, Jon M. "Korean Navy explored Ieodo in 1951." *Korea Times*, 29/06/2011. http://www.koreatimes.co.kr/www/news/nation/2012/02/359_89866.html

Van Dyke, Jon M. "The Republic of Korea's Maritime Boundaries," Honolulu, Hawaii: *William S. Richardson School of Law*, University of Hawaii at Manoa, 2003. http://webcache.googleusercontent.com/search?q=cache:F8E1lcIosdsJ:www.hawaii.edu/elp/publications/faculty/TheRepublicofKorea.doc+&cd=1&hl=ja&ct=clnk&gl=jp

Wada, Haruki. "Resolving the China-Japan Conflict Over the Senkaku/Diaoyu Islands." *History News Network*, 31/10/2010. http://www.hnn.us/articles/133059.html

Wang, Manna. "South Korea and China Conflict Over Islet in East China Sea." *Epoch Times*, 26/08/2007. https://www.theepochtimes.com/south-korea-and-china-conflict-over-islet-in-east-china-sea_1732773.html

Wang, Xiaobo. "Action, not protest, can save China's islands." *Global Times*, 16/01/2012. http://www.globaltimes.cn/content/692369.shtml

What China's Northeast Project Is All About (30/05/2008), *Chosun Ilbo*. http://english.chosun.com/site/data/html_dir/2008/05/30/2008053061001.html

Why China Would Compromise in the Yellow Sea (10/12/2015), *Stratfor Worldview*. https://www.stratfor.com/analysis/why-china-would-compromise-yellow-sea?utm_source=Twitter&utm_medium=Official&utm_campaign=Link

Yoon, Sukjoon. "Korea-China Maritime Boundary Talks: Implications for South China Sea." *RSIS Commentary* No. 89, 13 April 2015. https://www.rsis.edu.sg/wp-content/uploads/2015/04/CO15089.pdf

Yun, Yeongmi and Kicheol Park. "Structural Restrictions of Territorial Disputes In Northeast Asia," *Journal of East Asian Affairs* 27, no. 2 (Fall/Winter 2013): 89–117.

Zastrow, Mark. "Yellow Sea talks raise hopes for marine science," *Nature* 528 (15 December 2015). http://www.nature.com/news/yellow-sea-talks-raise-hopes-for-marine-science 1.19027

Zhang, Hongzhou. "China's Growing Fishing Industry and Regional Maritime Security," *S. Rajaratnam School of International Studies Commentaries* (2 June 2012). https://www.rsis.edu.sg/rsis-publication/idss/1753-chinas-growing-fishing-indu/#.WluGsq5l_Z4

Zhang, Yiqian. "Seoul expands KADIZ south." *Global Times*, 09/12/2013. http://www.globaltimes.cn/content/830911.shtml

Zhang, Yiqian. "S. Korea mulls expanding air zone further south." 28/11/2013. http://english.yonhapnews.co.kr/news/2013/11/28/22/0200000000AEN20131128009451315F.html

Zhang, Yunbi. "ROK's verdict on captain rejected." *China Daily*, 20/04/2012. http://wo.chinadaily.com.cn/view.php?mid=68604&cid=88&isid=809

Zhao, Jianming. "Cautious but firm attitude needed over Suyan Rock dispute with S. Korea." *Global Times*, 11/14/2012. http://www.globaltimes.cn/content/744314.shtml

Zhao, Quansheng. "China's Northeast Water Frontiers, East China Sea Disputes and Co-Management Approach." In: Hao, Yufan, and Bill K. P. Chou (eds.), *China's Policies on its Borderlands and the International Implications*. Singapore: World Scientific Publishing, 2011.

Zhen, Liu. "South Korea deploys new coastguard ship to watch waters around disputed Ieodo islet." *South China Morning Post*, 23/06/2016. http://www.scmp.com/news/china/diplomacy-defence/article/1979992/south-korea-deploys-new-coastguard-ship-watch-waters

Zhu, Jin. "Group Formed To Aid Fisheries." *China Daily*, 30/05/2012. http://usa.chinadaily.com.cn/china/2012-05/30/content_15418381.htm

Zou, Keyuan. "China's Exclusive Economic Zones and Continental Shelf: Developments, Problems, and Prospects," *Marine Policy* 25, no. 1 (2000): 71–81.

Index[1]

[1] Note: Page numbers followed by 'n' refer to notes.

S. Fox, *China, South Korea, and the Socotra Rock Dispute*,
https://doi.org/10.1007/978-981-13-2077-4

Printed by Printforce, the Netherlands